Insurance Accounting – Overview	2
Policy Maintenance Systems and the General Ledger	3
Reserves	3
Claims	5
Investment	6
Reinsurance	7
Pooling	8
Risk Based Capital (RBC)	9
Statutory versus GAAP	9
The Annual Statement – Overview	10
Pages, Exhibits, Schedules	12
Inputs to the Annual Statement	13
Importing Data	14
Attachments	15
Schedule P	16
Cash Flow	17
Validations	18
Filing and Submission	19
Signatures	19
State Filings	20
Premium Tax/Municipal Tax	20
Annual Statement Detail	21
Basic Accounting	28
Financial Statements, Recording Transactions, Accrual versus Cash	
Investment Accounting	33
Useful Formulas and Excel Techniques	46
Appendix	48

Insurance Accounting

This book is intended to fill a gap between too much information and too little. It is designed to give someone new to Insurance Accounting a comprehensive overview of the entire insurance accounting and NAIC Filing process. The topics and concepts presented have been taken from decades of helping insurance accountants complete their annual filings. They represent the common questions and uncertainties that people new to insurance accounting encounter. You can certainly get into more detail on specific insurance accounting issues but having a comprehensive overview will help speed up your training and jumpstart your insurance accounting career.

The book starts out with an Overview of some basic insurance concepts. The Annual Statement Detail section follows. It lists issues and information with specific statement pages. Then, there is a section on Basic Accounting and a section on Investment Accounting.

Overview

Insurance Accounting is one of the most exciting and challenging professions in accounting today. There are so many inputs from various systems that come together to produce a very comprehensive statement of financial position which is of utmost importance to policyholders and regulators. The Statutory Annual statement attempts to measure solvency, if the company was liquidated now, would the assets be adequate to pay off all current and future claims. Insurance policies contains a lot of information. Besides the basic contact and billing information, a policy might have Premium, Dividend, Policy Loan, Agent's Commission, Valuation and Claims records associated with it. Each of these records will interface with the general ledger over time. For instance, when a policy is sold, a premium is received, a commission paid and a reserve for future claims is setup. Each of these events causes changes to balances on the General Ledger and ultimately the Annual Statement.

Policy Maintenance Systems and the General Ledger

Every night and every month end, the computer systems at an insurance company run their nightly and monthly cycles. The daily cycle might summarize the premiums received or claims paid during the day and transfer that information to other systems like the Agency system that will accumulate then pay commissions on the premiums. Or it may transfer information to the Valuation system which adjusts the reserves for the policy. The transactions entered for the day will be summarized and entered into the General Ledger. The updates to the premium records on the policies will be reconciled back to the daily entry to the general ledger. Keeping everything reconciled so that you can run a report of all the Policy Loan balances on the policy records and tie that out to the Policy Loan account balance on the General Ledger is necessary and vital to the flow of information through the insurance company's financial reporting system. There are many systems that need to be kept reconciled to the general ledger. What if the 1099's produced at year end for the agent's commissions did not tie out to the commission expense in the general ledger? Do you think an agent that receives a 1099 showing more commission paid to him than he received would question the integrity of the general ledger and commission data?

Policy

The Policy systems will hold the detail to back up general ledger amounts such as the policy loan balance or the policy dividends unpaid balance. The Policy system has many tables that keep track of all the facets of a policy. Each policy has records in different tables which together describe the policy. Generally, every screen that you go into to view a policy represents a different record or partial record, associated with the policy. The individual data elements are the fields associated with the record in the table.

A database is comprised of multiple tables each with multiple records. The tables are linked by indexes so that you can query using the index value to pull all the data associated with a record from different tables.

Reserves

For life insurance, a reserve is set up using standard mortality tables and interest rates to determine the present value of the future claims payments that will be made. Usually the mortality rates and interest rates are determined by the assumptions used when the underlying policies were defined and approved for sale.

Life reserves are detailed in Exhibit 5 – Aggregate Reserve for Life Contracts. The reserves are scheduled out by Line of Business; Life, Annuity, Supplementary Contracts With Life Contingencies, Accidental Death, Disability and Miscellaneous and also by Type; Industrial, Ordinary, Credit and Group. The reserves are shown net of reinsurance. The summary from all the net reserves shown on Exhibit 5 are shown on line 1 of the Liabilities page. Life reserves are set up on a mean reserve basis. This is kind of an averaging method to value all the policies as of the middle of their policy year no matter when they were issued. Since policies are sold throughout the year, actuaries assume that all policies are issued on June 30th. Then they determine the December 31 reserve assuming that every policy has been in force for .5, 1.5, 2.5, 3.5, etc., years depending on the calendar year of issue. Thus the reserve at December 31 is approximated by taking the average of the reserve at the beginning of the policy year (initial) and the end of the policy year (terminal).

Mean Reserve = (Initial Reserve + Terminal Reserve) / 2

Because of this mean reserve valuation method, the company also needs to record net deferred premium and net uncollected premium assets to compensate for setting up the mean reserve. These assets offset the extra reserve liability which is set up for policies that have not yet paid their premium up to the mean reserve date.

On the Annual Statement, Uncollected Premiums are premiums whose due date was before December 31 but have not been collected yet. The grace period has not expired so the underlying policy is still in force. Uncollected premiums are shown on line 15.1 of the Asset page.

Deferred premiums will become due after December 31 but before the next anniversary date of the policy. Deferred premiums are shown on line 15.2 of the Asset page.

For example if a policy pays monthly premiums with an issue date of July 1, at year end, December 31, it may have not paid the December premium yet so 1 month of premium would be Uncollected (December) and 6 months of premium (January – June) would be Deferred.

Conversely, Unearned Premiums are liabilities set up to reflect the company's obligation to provide insurance in the future for premium income that has been received in advance. For example if a policy with an issue date of July 1 pays annually then at year end it would show 6 months of premiums as earned and 6 months of premium as Unearned. Unearned Premiums show up on the Liabilities page in the Advance Premiums line.

Claims

Claims reserves are maintained for claims that have been reported and claims that may have occurred but have not yet been reported. The reserve for claims that have been reported will be estimated as to the total cost that the insurance company is likely to incur. Similarly, the Incurred But Not Reported (IBNR) claims reserves are estimated based on past experience and average claim costs. An insurance company can track when the event causing the claim occurs and when the claim was actually reported to derive the IBNR claims.

Loss Reserves on a P&C statement are detailed on Part 2A – Unpaid Losses and Loss Adjustment Expenses. The total from Part 2A shows on Line 1 of the Liabilities page. Loss Adjustment Expenses are defined as the cost associated with settling and investigating and estimating the loss.

The Unpaid Losses on Part 2A are scheduled out to show the liability net of reinsurance. Direct Losses plus Assumed minus Ceded equals the Net Loss Liability excluding IBNR. To that number they add the Net Incurred But Not Reported (IBNR) to derive the Net Losses Unpaid which transfers to Part 2 column 5. Part 2 shows the Losses Paid and Incurred by line of business. Part 2 shows the Direct losses paid plus Assumed minus Ceded then adds the Net Losses Unpaid at year end from Part 2A minus the Beginning of the year Unpaid Losses to derive the Losses Incurred for the current year.

Incurred Losses = (Direct + Assumed – Ceded) + EOY Unpd – BOY Unpd

Investment

Investment reserves are unique to the insurance industry. Because of the assumptions made when designing an insurance policy, the regulators want to be sure the premium monies invested for a block of policies is kept invested to fund future claims on those same policies. When interest rates drop substantially, an insurance company can sell the older higher paying bonds for a substantial gain. Then they could use that gain to increase their surplus and as backing for new sales of other insurance policies. They could that is if the NAIC did not require them to set aside those gains and keep them as reserves specifically for the policies from which the initial premium monies were received!

The NAIC has set up an Interest Maintenance Reserve (IMR) and the Asset Valuation Reserve (AVR) and even a Risk Based Capital reserve (RBC) which is its own statement type.

The IMR is designed to capture the realized capital gains and losses that result from changes in the overall level of interest rates and amortize them into income over the approximate remaining life of the investment sold. Companies frequently maintain an Excel worksheet with the Gains and Losses from each year separated into its own row and then they amortize each row over 30 years for example. They add up the current year amortization from all the rows and that becomes their annual IMR Amortization that they are allowed to run through the income statement and close to surplus.

The AVR is designed to address the credit-related risks of the bonds and stocks by calculating a basic contribution, a reserve objective, and a maximum reserve amount. This reserve attempts to smooth the recognition of credit related gains and losses through surplus.

The Risk Based Capital (RBC) statement is a method of establishing the minimum amount of capital appropriate for an insurance company to support its overall business operations in consideration of its size and risk profile. It provides an elastic means of setting the minimum capital requirement in which the degree of risk taken by the insurer is the primary determinant.

A company's risk-based capital is calculated by applying factors to various asset, premium and reserve items. The factor is higher for those items with greater underlying risk and lower for less risky items. The adequacy of a company's actual capital may then be measured by a comparison to its risk-based capital as determined by the formula.

Risk-based capital standards will be used by regulators to set in motion appropriate regulatory actions relating to insurers that show indications of weak or deteriorating conditions. It also provides an additional standard for minimum capital requirements that companies should meet to avoid being placed in conservatorship.

Reinsurance

Insurance companies are rated every year by AM Best for example for many things, one of which is the adequacy of their reserves and surplus to fund the future claims. When insurance companies sell a lot of new business, they have to pay a lot of money up front for underwriting and first year commissions for example. All the first year expenses create a drain on surplus which can then cause their ratings to drop. So, insurance companies deliberately and carefully plan which policies they will sell in which areas of the country through which companies in order to generate the most revenue without draining their surplus so that ratings decline.

To maximize revenues across the entire organization, an insurance company might want to reinsure some of its costly new business from one of their younger lower surplus companies to one of their older surplus rich companies. That way they can maximize the use of their surplus across the organization to fund new business selling the most profitable insurance policies.

In addition to funding new policy sales on one company with the surplus from another company, insurers frequently transfer the excess risk to other companies to minimize their exposure to large claims. Many times a newer company with lower surplus will reinsure all its business over a certain dollar amount. For instance if a life insurance company sells a 300,000 dollar face value policy and it is only retaining 100,000 of risk, it will reinsure 200,000 to other reinsurance companies. It will then give the reinsurer 2/3 of the net premiums on the policy in return for their promise to pay 2/3 of all the claims on that policy. There are many different types of reinsurance agreements.

For instance, facultative reinsurance is a reinsurance policy that provides an insurer with coverage for specific individual risks that are unusual or so large that they aren't covered in the insurance company's reinsurance treaties.

This can include policies for jumbo jets or oil rigs for example. Reinsurers have no obligation to take on facultative reinsurance, but can assess each risk individually. By contrast, under treaty reinsurance, the reinsurer agrees to assume a certain percentage of entire classes of business, such as various kinds of auto, up to preset limits.

The premiums that are written on your company are called the Direct premiums. To transfer risk to another insurance company is called Ceding or Ceded. To assume the risk from another insurance company is called Assuming or Assumed.

To derive the income statement amounts net of reinsurance you would take your accrual basis direct premiums minus your ceded premiums plus your assumed premiums.

The reinsurance contract premium and claim amounts with individual reinsurers are detailed in Schedule F for PC and Schedule S for LAH. These schedules give detail to back up the summary reinsurance amounts used in other schedules.

Pooling

Pooling is a reinsurance arrangement among affiliated companies, where the subject business written by the pool participants is ceded to the pool lead then retro-ceded among pool participants according to a specified percentage of the total.

The complexity in a pooling arrangement is to report the claims history on schedule P accurately. If the pool percentages change, then the prior year claims activity must be restated so that the claims history will be reported properly.

Generally, the prior year statements and the current year claims activity roll up into a Sum of Pool statement. The Schedule P information is taken from the Sum of Pool using the current pooling percentages. Prior year links to accumulate the Non-Schedule P data are then used to complete the remainder of the statement and create the Filed NAIC Statement.

Risk Based Capital (RBC)

The RBC statement is a statement associated with a specific Annual Statement for a specific company. The RBC judges the adequacy of the surplus for the company. It looks at the quality of the investment, rate of premium growth, claims history and assigns factors used to compute the required capital. If a company grows too quickly for example, the Excess Premium Growth schedule would assign a bigger factor and require more surplus. If the investment portfolio had an inordinate amount of low quality bonds, a larger factor would be assigned requiring more capital. The actual surplus is compared to the RBC computed surplus and depending on how it compares, might bring about greater scrutiny from the regulators.

In addition to the Bond and Stock quality sections there is also a Concentration Factor section where all the investments in a company are compared. Not counting US Government bonds, the top holdings for a company are scheduled out and given a reserve factor based on their investment quality. Typically the first 6 digits of the cusip number will identify the company issuing the investment so you can subtotal all investments by this to determine the asset concentration amounts.

Statutory versus GAAP

Statutory (STAT) insurance accounting can be thought of as more conservative than Generally Accepted Accounting Principles (GAAP) accounting. GAAP is more of a "going concern" approach whereas STAT is more of a "solvency" approach. GAAP is probably a more realistic measure of how profitable an insurance company is than STAT. For instance in GAAP the costs of acquiring new business such as underwriting and first year commissions are capitalized and amortized to expense over several years. This represents more of a matching approach to revenue recognition. These costs are called Deferred Acquisition Costs, (DAC). Also, bonds will be valued at their fair value for GAAP rather than their amortized cost like STAT usually does.

GAAP policy reserves will be computed differently from STAT reserves. Companies can use their experience to assign interest rates and mortality rates that can be different from those prescribed by STAT.

Policyholder dividends are recorded as liabilities in STAT when they are declared by the Board of Directors. Under GAAP, dividends are assumed to be payable based on experience and intent and are accrued even without a declaration by the Board of Directors.

GAAP accounting will record Deferred Income Taxes to recognize timing differences between the tax return and the ultimate tax liability. STAT does not require recognition of Deferred Income Taxes although many companies do have this on their STAT statements. Just know that there is a difference in calculation between STAT and GAAP for Deferred Income Taxes.

GAAP does not Non-Admit assets like STAT accounting does.

The Annual Statement - Overview

The annual statement today looks similar to the annual statements from the 1920s except the numbers are not hand written anymore! Generally, an annual statement is a uniform financial statement with many Exhibits and Schedules to show the results of operations in great detail. The exhibits and schedules show the results of operations by line of business and net of reinsurance transactions.

The output from the Annual Statement is compiled into a .Zip file that includes several .PDF files and a couple .txt files. The PDF files are organized into a Key pages (PK), Investment pages (PI) and Other pages (PO). There is one big .txt file that ends in _s.txt. It contains all the data from all the pages in the standard NAIC Filing layout. It is a tab delimited text file. There is also a validations file in the .Zip file. The .Zip file is uploaded to the NAIC website. Here are the files included in the zip file.

- 12345_38_P_2012_O_M_1_00_NA_E.TXT
- 12345_38_P_2012_O_M_1_00_NA_PA.PDF
- 12345_38_P_2012_O_M_1_00_NA_PI.PDF
- 12345_38_P_2012_O_M_1_00_NA_PK.PDF
- 12345_38_P_2012_O_M_1_00_NA_PO.PDF
- 12345_38_P_2012_O_M_1_00_NA_S.TXT
- 12345_38_P_2012_O_M_1_00_NA_V.TXT

The 12345 is the NAIC Company Code. The P_2012_O_M_1 represents P&C, 2012 Original March Filing number 1.

Your General Ledger numbers for Assets, Liabilities, Retained Earnings and Income Statement are all fully reported on the first three pages. Amounts from the Income Statement are then further broken out by the Exhibits which follow. For instance Losses Incurred on line 2 of the Statement of Income on a PC statement is detailed on the Underwriting and Expense Exhibit Part 2 – Losses Paid and Incurred. Part 2 has about 30 different lines of business and schedules out the Direct and Assumed and the beginning and ending Unpaid amounts to derive the Incurred losses for the current year.

The *_S.TXT file is created in the NAIC Annual Uniform Layout which most of the Investment programs write out. It looks like this where each new page/identifier starts with a square bracketed header row to identify which page the following data represents. The first column is the line type indicator, D for Detail, I for Inset. The second column is the Line Number and the leading zero is necessary. Line number "01" does not equate to line number "1".

[P2012ASSETS]					
D	01	31451033	0	31451033	35459787
D	02.1	0	0	0	0
D	02.2	182330	0	182330	165179
D	03.1	0	0	0	0
D	03.2	0	0	0	0
D	04.1	832974	0	832974	852272
I	04.1	0			
D	04.2	0	0	0	0
I	04.2	0			
D	04.3	0	0	0	0
I	04.3	0			
D	05	10610016	0	10610016	5152752
I	05	179925	0	10430091	
D	06	0	0	0	0
I	06	0			
D	07	0	0	0	0
D	08	0	0	0	0

Pages, Exhibits and Schedules

Amounts on the Assets and Liabilities pages are also more fully detailed on different schedules then totaled and transferred to the balance sheet. On the P&C Liabilities page for example, many of the loss and reinsurance liabilities come from the many schedule F parts. On the assets page many of the bond and stock totals come from schedule D pages.

In the Exhibits and Schedules, you will see cash basis expenses converted to accrual basis. Expenses incurred on an accrual basis equals the cash basis expenses paid less the beginning of the year accruals plus the end of the year accruals. Some of the cash basis expenses paid during the year pay off the expenses incurred on an accrual basis last year so they are not current year expenses.

Also you see the premiums and claims scheduled out net of reinsurance as the direct business plus the assumed less the ceded equals the net premiums or net claims.

Many of the schedules and exhibits break out the results of operations by line of business. Usually the general ledger account numbers incorporate the line of business as a substring imbedded into the account numbers. Reports can be generated showing the premium, commissions and claims by line of business using report generating software that sorts by the line of business codes in the account numbers.

Another thing you will see in the annual statement is the non-admitting of assets. The exhibit of non-admitted assets decreases the amount that can be recognized on the Assets page for certain assets due to a high probability it is uncollectible or excess risk of default for example. An increase in the non-admitted assets is an expense that is taken to the surplus section of the income statement. This also has to be added back to the cash flow page as discussed later.

One last thing you need to understand in an annual statement is the recognition of unrealized gains and losses. The NAIC has a table in the schedule D1 instructions that sets forth when a bond must be valued at the lower of book or fair based on the NAIC Designation. If a bond is valued at Fair then there will be an amount shown in the unrealized column. The Unrealized column is only for the current year adjustment. It is not life to date. When a bond that was valued at fair last year end is sold for a loss this year, the schedules need to show a reversal of the unrealized loss from prior years in order to recognize the full amount of the realized loss this year. Many people think the reversal of the Unrealized should include the current year change in unrealized also but, if you look at the formula for the Verification Between Periods schedule you will see that is not correct. Unrealized losses would also need to be added back to the cash flow page as discussed later.

Inputs to the Annual Statement

The annual statement has many inputs. Certainly the adjusted trial balance from the General Ledger is a main source. Many general ledgers have lines of business codes inherent in their account numbering structure. Also, the account numbers frequently have the assumed and ceded reinsurance codes built into the account numbers. The first three pages could be loaded from the trial balance except that many of the cells on those pages actually pull from Exhibits and Schedules further down in the statement.

The Valuation system is another main source of input into the annual statement. It is where all the policy reserve amounts and counts come from. In the LAH statement the reserves are reported on Exhibit 5. In the PC statement the Loss reserves show up on part 2A.

The Claims system also is used extensively to fill out annual statement exhibits. Claims paid and unpaid are scheduled out on Exhibit 8 for LAH statements and Exhibit 2 on PC statements.

Results of operations are also allocated to states and a separate state page is created showing the results of operations by line of business within each state.

Investment systems are responsible for importing much of the data necessary for the investment schedules like all the Schedule D reports for the bonds and stocks. The D reports show the year end carrying value of the assets which may be either the amortized cost or the fair value based on the company type and the NAIC designation. The D reports allocate and report all the amortization and interest income by the par value outstanding during the year. If a mortgage backed bond pays a redemption amount or if a partial sale is recorded, the amortization and interest attributable to that redemption or partial sale must be allocated to it based on the number of days that par value was held for the year.

General expenses are detailed by type and also split to general lines of business. The Analysis of Operations by Line of Business is basically a statement of income for each line of business. The Analysis of Operations by line of Business splits everything from premium and claims to investment income and expenses and taxes across the different lines of business. Sometimes an insurance company completes a Functional Cost Survey to help them allocate fixed costs by line of business based on how much time certain departments spend on certain tasks.

The NAIC has set up Validations and EagleTM has added their own validations to help you balance out the statement. For instance, line 1 of the Liabilities page is labeled Losses and it must tie to the bottom line of Exhibit 2A which breaks out the Losses liability by line of business showing reinsurance activity also. If these two amounts do not equal a validation rule will fail. If the difference is more than NAIC allows it to be off, the validation is said to be Out Of Tolerance (OOT). If the difference is less than the NAIC allows then it is Out Of Balance (OOB). All OOT must be either cleared by correcting something or explained by entering an explanation. EagleTM validations will never be OOT, if they fail they will show up as OOB.

Importing Data

Because the NAIC filing file is such a well-known and accepted format, many systems are designed to create that format and annual statement programs are designed to import files in that format. All the investment accounting programs now create the files to be imported in the NAIC filing format, sometimes called the Annual uniform layout. This is a Tab-Delimited Text file opened in Excel using the Text-Import Wizard. Text files are not the same as Word or PDF files. You can't import Word or PDF files.

```
                 --------
[P2012SCDPT2SN1]
D                8499999
D                8599999
D                8999999
[P2012SCDPT2SN2]
D                9000001  117043    10   9   BRUNSWICK CORPORATION                                    1000     29090    29.09
D                9000002  486587    10   8   KAYDON CORPORATION                                        500     11965    23.93
D                9000003  655844    10   8   NORFOLK SOUTHERN CORPORATION                              600     37104    61.84
D                9000004  90390U    10   2   SLM CORPORATION                                           900     15417    17.13
D                9000005  939640    10   8   WASHINGTON POST CO - CLASS B                               55     20087   365.21
D                9000006  949746    10   1   WELLS FARGO AND COMPANY                                  2009     68668    34.18
D                9099999                                                                                      182330
D                9199999                                                                                           0
D                9299999                                                                                           0
D                9399999                                                                                           0
D                9799999                                                                                      182330
D                9899999                                                                                      182330
[P2012SCDPT2SN2F]
D                0000001  0         0
[P2012SCDPT3]
D                0599999                                                                                                 0
D                1099999                                                                                                 0
D                1700001  01179P    QQ   3   ALASKA, MUNICIPAL BOND BANK AI   7252012  FOLGER NOLAN FLEMING DOUGLAS  165278
D                1700002  341535    RM   6   FLORIDA, STATE BRD ED PUB ED CAP 1232012  FOLGER NOLAN FLEMING DOUGLAS  108824
D                1700003  73358T    FT   3   NEW YORK & NEW JERSEY, PORT AU   9112012  FOLGER NOLAN FLEMING DOUGLAS  106117
D                1700004  73358T    QB   0   NEW YORK & NEW JERSEY, PORT AU   8032012  FOLGER NOLAN FLEMING DOUGLAS   21920
D                1700005  73358T    V4   0   NEW YORK & NEW JERSEY, PORT AU   9182012  FOLGER NOLAN FLEMING DOUGLAS   34366
D                1700006  73358T    U5   8   NEW YORK & NEW JERSEY, PORT AU   9062012  FOLGER NOLAN FLEMING DOUGLAS   40954
D                1799999                                                                                             477459
```

There are many other methods to import data into the Annual Statement. Methods ranging from specialized Excel worksheets to .XML files are used. Typically, a company might cell reference their Excel Data into an accepted format for importing if it can be done by simply copying blocks of formulas. Then the properly formatted data is saved as a Text, Tab-Delimited file and that is the file that is imported into the Annual Statement.

Blocks of data can usually be copied and pasted into the annual statement pages also.

Attachments

There are many attachments like the Notes to Financials and the Organization Chart where you need to submit both a printable image and also the electronic data. The electronic data is usually typed into a page whereas the printable image would be attached in a ready to print format.

Some attachments like the Audited Financial statement are submitted as PDF files with no electronic data component. The NAIC uses a program to read the PDF and look for sensitive data which they would not want to publish. If you submit a protected PDF, their program cannot search within the file and they will ask you to resubmit the file in an unprotected state.

Schedule P

Schedule P is a PC Claims schedule which is organized by Accident year. So if a claim occurred in 2005 and payments were made on that claim in each of the next three years, you would see the cumulative paid amounts at the end of each calendar year for the claim arising in 2005. Generally, you only need to import or enter the claims paid in the current year and you would spread them across the accident years they originated in. The prior year claims data would remain the same except for it would be shifted up one and over one to match the new rows and columns on the current year statement. The prior year data plus the current year data is combined to create the published data. The published data for each line of business is then summarized for all lines of business.

Most lines of business in Schedule P have 10 years history and there is also a Prior line. The Prior line represents only claim payments made in the 10 reported years for accident years prior to the reported years. Many companies mistakenly report the cumulative paid losses for prior accident years on the prior line.

Some of the lines of business are called "Short Tail Lines" which means that they do not have all 10 years of history broken out into 10 rows. Some of the accident years are combined to report a summary of many accident years. Typically when companies switch annual statement providers, prior year's statements are loaded from the NAIC Filing files which do not have all 10 years' worth of data for the short tail lines. Usually, short tail lines schedules on the prior year statement which was loaded from the filing file will need to expanded to break out the summarized prior line into all 10 years in order to make the current year statement calculate correctly.

SCHEDULE P - PART 2 - SUMMARY

Years in Which Losses Were Incurred	INCURRED NET LOSSES AND DEFENSE AND COST CONTAINMENT EXPENSES REPORTED AT YEAR END ($000 OMITTED)										
	1 2003	2 2004	3 2005	4 2006	5 2007	6 2008	7 2009	8 2010	9 2011	10 2012
1. Prior	0	0	0	0	0	0	0	0	0	0
2. 2003	142,744	125,228	108,818	106,709	107,394	107,952	107,635	109,607	110,089	103,865
3. 2004	XXX	244,179	227,543	219,167	217,688	210,633	209,610	201,872	218,093	208,489
4. 2005	XXX	XXX	445,065	416,597	401,525	389,675	390,384	390,515	443,758	426,898
5. 2006	XXX	XXX	XXX	427,065	401,552	383,069	383,583	372,233	411,559	418,559
6. 2007	XXX	XXX	XXX	XXX	509,370	486,428	484,382	473,774	524,055	525,462
7. 2008	XXX	XXX	XXX	XXX	XXX	518,614	501,793	487,395	578,068	564,547
8. 2009	XXX	XXX	XXX	XXX	XXX	XXX	485,523	462,272	545,205	576,971
9. 2010	XXX	XXX	XXX	XXX	XXX	XXX	XXX	544,853	703,332	670,249
10. 2011	XXX	XXX	XXX	XXX	XXX	XXX	XXX	XXX	780,895	823,601
11. 2012	XXX	XXX	XXX	XXX	XXX	XXX	XXX	XXX	XXX	685,588

Cash Flow - The cash flow statement is usually one of the last pages to be completed because it depends on many of the other pages. The cash flow is really quite mechanical. Completing it is simply a matter of tying out all the changes in all the Assets, Liabilities and then including the Net Income and adding back any non-cash income/expense items such as Amortization and Depreciation for example. The change in cash has to equal the cash basis change in all the other Assets, Liabilities and Net income.

Sometimes you actually have to trace the difference in each line item on the balance sheet to the cash flow work-paper in order to get the cash flow to balance to the change in cash. You should use a sources and uses approach. An increase in an asset is a use of cash, to buy a new machine for example. A decrease in an asset is a source of cash, to sell a stock for example. An increase in a liability is a source of cash, to take out a loan for example. A decrease in a liability is a use of cash, to pay off a loan for example. A non cash income item such as discount amortization on a bond is initially recorded as income but needs to be added back because it is not a source of cash. Similarly, the depreciation on a fixed asset is recorded as an expense but must be added back because it did not require the outlay of cash. See Workpaper below.

Cash Flow

		1 Current Year	2 Prior Year	3 Change	4 Sources (Uses)	5 Amount
01.100	P4 L1 Premiums earned	410,528,783			410,528,783	
01.200	P2 L15.1 Uncollected Premiums and Agents Balances in course of Collection	52,398,281	43,119,791	9,278,490	(9,278,490)	
01.201	P2 L15.2 Deferred Premium and Agents Balances not yet due.	1,164,941,278	1,323,454,388	(158,513,110)	158,513,110	
01.202	P2 L15.3 Accrued Retrospective Premium	5,700,126	4,092,026	1,608,100	(1,608,100)	
01.203	KEY P2 L16.2 (in part for amount related to earned premiums)	72,608,275	45,894,108	26,714,167	(26,714,167)	
01.204	KEY P2 L16.3 (in part for experience rating and other amounts related to earned premiums)	0	0	0	0	
01.300	P3 L9 Unearned Premiums	491,631,595	475,810,148	15,821,447	15,821,447	
01.301	P3 L10 Advance Premiums	0	0	0	0	
01.302	P3 L12 Ceded Reinsurance Premium Payable	220,409,000	794,012,643	(573,603,643)	(573,603,643)	
01.401	ADJUSTMENTS as Income				0	
01.499	Total Adjustments					
01.500	Total Line 1 Premiums Collected net of Reinsurance				(26,341,060)	(26,341,060)
02.100	Page 4 L9 Net investment					

Validations

Some validations check for totals between pages that should tie out if the numbers flow through the statement correctly. Some validations check the totals on the page to make sure they equal the detail. Some validations check for the presence of data when a condition is met. The General Interrogatories ask question such as will this schedule or that one be filed? If you answer yes to one of those questions and that schedule is not completed you would see a crosscheck warning of the inconsistency.

The cross checks that check for two numbers being equal to each other are presented only once, usually on the page that is closer to the front of the statement. The screen shot below shows the Assets Page and its associated Validation Errors. You read the formulas as Page, Line Column references with the associated amounts.

		1	2	3	4
	Assets	Assets	Nonadmitted Assets	Net Admitted Assets (Cols. 1 - 2)	Prior Year: Net Admitted Assets
01.	Bonds (Schedule D)	2,224,332,91	0	2,224,332,91	2,236,436,03
02.1	Preferred stocks (Schedule D)	0	0	0	0
02.2	Common stocks (Schedule D)	615,446,435	0	615,446,435	634,303,729
03.1	Mortgage loans on real estate: First liens	0	0	0	0
03.2	Mortgage loans on real estate: Other than first liens	0	0	0	0
04.1	Properties occupied by the company (less $... encumbrances)	0	0	0	0
04.2	Properties held for the production of income (less $... encumbrances)	0	0	0	0
04.3	Properties held for sale (less $... encumbrances)	0	0	0	0
05.	Cash ($..., Schedule E Part 1), cash equivalents ($..., Schedule E Part 2) and short-term investments ($..., Schedule DA)	332,529,756	0	332,529,756	275,986,794
06.	Contract loans (including $... premium notes)	0	0	0	0
07.	Derivatives (Schedule DB)	0	0	0	0
08.	Other invested assets (Schedule BA)	0	0	0	0
09.	Receivables for securities	104,022	0	104,022	193,332
10.	Securities lending reinvested collateral assets (Schedule DL)	0	0	0	0
11.	Aggregate write-ins for invested assets	0	0	0	0
12.	Subtotals, cash and invested assets (Lines 1 to 11)	3,172,413,12	0	3,172,413,12	3,146,919,88
13.	Title plants less $... Charged off (for Title insurers only)	0	0	0	0

xplanation	Rule	Left Formula	Left Value	Right Formula	Right Value	Difference
	PIASU095177	[P2012ASSETS, 05, 3] [332,529,756]	332,529,756.00	[P2012ASSETS, 05, I1] [132,774,785] +[P2012ASSETS, 05, I2] [7,847,123] +[P2012ASSETS, 05, I3] [21,764,543]	162,386,451.00	170,143,305
	PTASU092014	(ASSETS - 2501 Missing Write-ins Descriptions	0		0	
	PXASN000040	[P2012ASSETS, 16.2, 3] [72,608,275] / 1,000	72,608.28	[P2012SCFPT1, 9999999, 12] [55,744]	55,743.65	16,864.623
	PXASN000042	[P2012ASSETS, 16.1, 3] [55,212,989]	55,212,989.00	[P2012HIST6YR, 20.1, 1] [52,393,511]	52,393,511.00	2,819,478
	PXASN000043	[P2012ASSETS, 15.2, 3] [943,142,498]	943,142,498.00	[P2012HIST6YR, 20.2, 1] [1,164,941,278]	1,164,941,278.00	221,798,78
	PXASN000044	[P2012ASSETS, 15.3, 3] [8,933,720]	8,933,720.00	[P2012HIST6YR, 20.3, 1] [5,700,126]	5,700,126.00	3,233,594
	PXASN000048	[P2012ASSETS, 16.1, 3] [278,519,013] / 1,000	278,519.01	[P2012SCFPT3, 9999999, 7] [284,509] +[P2012SCFPT3, 9999999, 8] [14,872]	299,381.36	20,862.347
	PXASN000051	[P2012ASSETS, 16.1, 3] [278,519,013] / 1,000	278,519.01	[P2012SCFPT4, 9999999, 11] [299,383]	299,383.32	20,864.307

Filing and Submission

There are annual filing requirements for March 1st, that is the big one, and smaller filing requirements for April 1 and June 1.

The March 1st filing includes most of the statement plus the Actuarial Opinion, Reinsurance Attestation, etc. The April 1st filing includes the Policy Experience Exhibits, the Management Discussion and Analysis and the Supplemental Health Care exhibit. The June 1st filing includes the Audited Financials and the Accountant's Letter of Qualifications.

Signatures

Companies usually only provide a hard copy of the annual statement to their state of domicile. A word to the wise about signatures….. Signing the Jurat page is done on the completed statements after you get them back from printing, usually right before the due date. However, the executives that need to sign will most likely be out of the office on business at that time. Therefore, many companies print out the signature section of the Jurat page on a large sticker sheet and have the executives sign that before the books come back from printing. Then they can simply affix the signatures sticker to the printed Jurat page and be ready to file.

State Filings

Every state that a company does business in has their own two dozen forms or so that are specific to that state. Those forms are enumerated on the State Checklist which is a form common to all states. EagleTM maintains a library of all these forms from every state. They drop form fields on the actual state forms so that the forms will pre-populate with the data from the annual statement. It is usually the balance sheet, company information, state pages and schedule T that have the data which is used to auto-complete these forms. The remainder of the fields can simply be entered manually and then all the fields are saved to a database so you can re-open the form later and see all the data.

Premium Tax

Insurance companies have to pay premium taxes to the states where they write their business. EagleTM keeps a library of all the premium tax forms for every state. The tax forms will prepopulate with annual statement data automatically. The form data is saved into a database and the forms automatically calculate the tax liability.

Municipal Tax

Within a state, municipalities will charge a tax on premiums written in their geographical location. EagleTM has both a library of municipal tax forms and a geocoding program to help insurance companies determine which municipality the insured policy resides in.

Annual Statement Detail

There is a complete list of the Annual Statement pages in Appendix A.

The Assets, Liabilities and Summary of Operations pages are shown in detail here so you can see where all the Exhibits and Schedules transfer in their numbers. The Assets page is the same for LAH and PC so it is only presented once.

Life Accident and Health – Assets (There are Ledger, Non-Admitted and Net Admitted columns)

- 01 Bonds (Schedule D1) – (The Carrying value column on D1 is usually the amortized cost or book value but it can be the fair value for TIPS bonds and lower quality bonds, see investment section below.)
- 02.1 Preferred stocks (Schedule D2.1) – (The carrying value column on D2.1 is usually the cost or fair value depending on whether the stock is Redeemable or Perpetual. The NAIC designations of RP or PP relate to Reedemable Pref or Perpetual Pref.)
- 02.2 Common stocks (Schedule D2.2) – The carrying value is always the fair value
- 03.1 Mortgage loans on real estate: First liens – Reported on (Sch B)
- 03.2 Mortgage loans on real estate: Other than first liens (Sch B)
- 04.1 Properties occupied by the company (less $... encumbrances) (Sch A)
- 04.2 Properties held for the production of income (less $... encumbrances) (Sch A)
- 04.3 Properties held for sale (less $... encumbrances) (Reported Sch A)
- 05 Cash ($..., Schedule E Part 1), cash equivalents ($..., Schedule E Part 2) and short-term investments ($..., Schedule DA)
  (E1 is bank deposits, E2 is cash equivalents and investments maturing in 3 months or less and not money markets, DA1 is for investments maturing in 1 year or less from date of purchase.)
- 06 Contract loans (including $... premium notes) (includes Policy Loans)
- 07 Derivatives (Schedule DB) (options, puts and calls from hedging transactions)
- 08 Other invested assets (Schedule BA)
- 09 Receivables for securities
- 10 Securities lending reinvested collateral assets (Schedule DL)
- 11 Aggregate write-ins for invested assets
- 12 Subtotals, cash and invested assets (Lines 1 to 11)
- 13 Title plants less $... Charged off (for Title insurers only)
- 14 Investment income due and accrued (Net Investment Income Exh.)
- 15.1 Uncollected premiums and agents' balances in the course of collection (defined above)
- 15.2 Deferred premiums, agents' balances and installments booked but deferred and not yet due (including $... earned but unbilled premiums) (Defined above)
- 15.3 Accrued retrospective premiums – (A retrospective premium policy, unlike a standard insurance policy, provides for retrospective determination of the policyholder's premium obligations according to a formula based on the cost of claims actually paid by the insurance company under the policy.)
- 16.1 Amounts recoverable from reinsurers
- 16.2 Funds held by or deposited with reinsured companies
- 16.3 Other amounts receivable under reinsurance contracts
- 17 Amounts receivable relating to uninsured plans

18.1 Current federal and foreign income tax recoverable and interest thereon
18.2 Net deferred tax asset – (Deferred tax assets can arise due to net loss carry-overs, which are only recorded as assets if it is deemed more likely than not that the asset will be used in future fiscal periods.)
19 Guaranty funds receivable or on deposit
20 Electronic data processing equipment and software
21 Furniture and equipment, including health care delivery assets ($ ...)
22 Net adjustment in assets and liabilities due to foreign exchange rates
23 Receivables from parent, subsidiaries and affiliates (The payable on the parent's financial statement should equal the receivable here!)
24 Health care ($ ...) and other amounts receivable
25 Aggregate write-ins for other than invested assets
26 Total assets excluding Separate Accounts, Segregated Accounts and Protected Cell Accounts (Lines 12 to 25)
27 From Separate Accounts, Segregated Accounts and Protected Cell Accounts
28 Total (Lines 26 and 27)

Life Accident and Health – Liabilities

01 Aggregate reserve for life contracts $... (Exh. 5, Line 9999999) less $... included in Line 6.3 (including $... Modco Reserve)
02 Aggregate reserve for accident and health contracts (including $... Modco Reserve)
03 Liability for deposit-type contracts (Exhibit 7, Line 14, Col. 1) (including $... Modco Reserve)
04.1 Life (Exhibit 8, Part 1, Line 4.4, Col. 1 less sum of Cols. 9, 10 and 11)
04.2 Accident and health (Exhibit 8, Part 1, Line 4.4, sum of Cols. 9, 10 and 11)
05 Policyholders' dividends $... and coupons $... due and unpaid (Exhibit 4, Line 10)
06.1 Dividends apportioned for payment (including $... Modco)
06.2 Dividends not yet apportioned (including $... Modco)
06.3 Coupons and similar benefits (including $... Modco)
07 Amount provisionally held for deferred dividend policies not included in Line 6
08 Premiums and annuity considerations for life and accident and health contracts received in advance less $... discount; including $... accident and health premiums (Exhibit 1, Part 1, Col. 1, sum of lines 4 and 14)
09.1 Surrender values on canceled contracts
09.2 Provision for experience rating refunds, including the liability of $... accident and health experience rating refunds of which $... is for medical loss ratio rebate per the Public Health Service Act
09.3 Other amounts payable on reinsurance, including $... assumed and $... ceded
09.4 Interest maintenance reserve (IMR, Line 6)
10 Commissions to agents due or accrued-life and annuity contracts $... accident and health $... and deposit-type contract funds $...
11 Commissions and expense allowances payable on reinsurance assumed
12 General expenses due or accrued (Exhibit 2, Line 12, Col. 6)
13 Transfers to Separate Accounts due or accrued (net) (including $... accrued for expense allowances recognized in reserves, net of reinsured allowances)
14 Taxes, licenses and fees due or accrued, excluding federal income taxes (Exhibit 3, Line 9, Col. 5)
15.1 Current federal and foreign income taxes, including $... on realized capital gains (losses)

15.2	Net deferred tax liability – (A deferred tax liability arises when a company's real-world tax bill is lower than what its financial statements suggest it should be due to differences between tax accounting rules and standard accounting practices. The liability signals to observers that the company remains under a tax obligation.)
16	Unearned investment income (received in advance, not yet earned)
17	Amounts withheld or retained by company as agent or trustee
18	Amounts held for agents' account, including $... agents' credit balances
19	Remittances and items not allocated
20	Net adjustment in assets and liabilities due to foreign exchange rates
21	Liability for benefits for employees and agents if not included above
22	Borrowed money $... and interest thereon $...
23	Dividends to stockholders declared and unpaid
24.01	Asset valuation reserve (AVR, Line 16, Col. 7)(defined above)
24.02	Reinsurance in unauthorized and certified ($...) companies
24.03	Funds held under reinsurance treaties with unauthorized and certified ($...) reinsurers
24.04	Payable to parent, subsidiaries and affiliates
24.05	Drafts outstanding
24.06	Liability for amounts held under uninsured plans
24.07	Funds held under coinsurance
24.08	Derivatives
24.09	Payable for securities
24.10	Payable for securities lending
24.11	Capital notes $... and interest thereon $...
25	Aggregate write-ins for liabilities
26	Total liabilities excluding Separate Accounts business (Lines 1 to 25)
27	From Separate Accounts Statement
28	Total liabilities (Lines 26 and 27)
29	Common capital stock
30	Preferred capital stock
31	Aggregate write-ins for other than special surplus funds
32	Surplus notes
33	Gross paid in and contributed surplus (Page 3, Line 33, Col. 2 plus Page 4, Line 51.1, Col. 1)
34	Aggregate write-ins for special surplus funds
35	Unassigned funds (surplus)
36.1	Treasury stock at cost: common
36.2	Treasury stock at cost: preferred
37	Surplus (Total Lines 31+32+33+34+35-36) (including $... in Separate Accounts Statement)
38	Totals of Lines 29, 30 and 37 (Page 4, Line 55)
39	Totals of Lines 28 and 38 (Page 2, Line 28,Col. 3)

Life Accident and Health – Summary of Operations – (many items should tie to the summary column on Analysis of Operations by Line of Business)

01	Premiums and annuity considerations for life and accident and health contracts (Exhibit 1, Part 1, Line 20.4, Col. 1, less Col. 11)
02	Considerations for supplementary contracts with life contingencies
03	Net investment income (Exhibit of Net Investment Income, Line 17)

04	Amortization of Interest Maintenance Reserve (IMR, Line 5) (defined above)
05	Separate Accounts net gain from operations excluding unrealized gains or losses
06	Commissions and expense allowances on reinsurance ceded (Exhibit 1, Part 2, Line 26.1, Col. 1)
07	Reserve adjustments on reinsurance ceded
08.1	Income from fees associated with investment management, administration and contract guarantees from Separate Accounts
08.2	Charges and fees for deposit-type contracts
08.3	Aggregate write-ins for miscellaneous income
09	Totals (Lines 1 to 8.3)
10	Death benefits
11	Matured endowments (excluding guaranteed annual pure endowments)
12	Annuity benefits (Exhibit 8, Part 2, Line 6.4, Cols. 4 + 8)
13	Disability benefits and benefits under accident and health contracts
14	Coupons, guaranteed annual pure endowments and similar benefits
15	Surrender benefits and withdrawals for life contracts
16	Group conversions
17	Interest and adjustments on contract or deposit-type contract funds
18	Payments on supplementary contracts with life contingencies
19	Increase in aggregate reserves for life and accident and health contracts
20	Totals (Lines 10 to 19)
21	Commissions on premiums, annuity considerations, and deposit-type contract funds (direct business only) (Exhibit 1, Part 2, Line 31, Col. 1)
22	Commissions and expense allowances on reinsurance assumed (Exhibit 1, Part 2, Line 26.2, Col. 1)
23	General insurance expenses (Exhibit 2, Line 10, Cols. 1, 2, 3 and 4)
24	Insurance taxes, licenses and fees, excluding federal income taxes (Exhibit 3, Line 7, Cols. 1 + 2 + 3)
25	Increase in loading on deferred and uncollected premiums
26	Net transfers to or (from) Separate Accounts net of reinsurance
27	Aggregate write-ins for deductions
28	Totals (Lines 20 to 27)
29	Net gain from operations before dividends to policyholders and federal income taxes (Line 9 minus Line 28)
30	Dividends to policyholders
31	Net gain from operations after dividends to policyholders and before federal income taxes (Line 29 minus Line 30)
32	Federal and foreign income taxes incurred (excluding tax on capital gains)
33	Net gain from operations after dividends to policyholders and federal income taxes and before realized capital gains or (losses) (Line 31 minus Line 32)
34	Net realized capital gains (losses) (excluding gains (losses) transferred to the IMR) less capital gains tax of $... (excluding taxes of $... transferred to the IMR)
35	Net income (Line 33 plus Line 34)
36	Capital and surplus, December 31, prior year (Page 3, Line 38, Col. 2)
37	Net income (Line 35)
38	Change in net unrealized capital gains (losses) less capital gains tax of $...
39	Change in net unrealized foreign exchange capital gain (loss)
40	Change in net deferred income tax
41	Change in nonadmitted assets (Exhibit of Non Admits)
42	Change in liability for reinsurance in unauthorized and certified companies

43 Change in reserve on account of change in valuation basis, (increase) or decrease (ExchgVal)
44 Change in asset valuation reserve (AVR)
45 Change in treasury stock (Page 3, Lines 36.1 and 36.2, Col. 2 minus Col. 1)
46 Surplus (contributed to) withdrawn from Separate Accounts during period
47 Other changes in surplus in Separate Accounts Statement
48 Change in surplus notes
49 Cumulative effect of changes in accounting principles
50.1 Capital changes: Paid in
50.2 Capital changes: Transferred from surplus (Stock Dividend)
50.3 Capital changes: Transferred to surplus
51.1 Surplus adjustment: Paid in
51.2 Surplus adjustment: Transferred to capital (Stock Dividend)
51.3 Surplus adjustment: Transferred from capital
51.4 Change in surplus as a result of reinsurance
52 Dividends to stockholders
53 Aggregate write-ins for gains and losses in surplus
54 Net change in capital and surplus for the year (Lines 37 through 53)
55 Capital and surplus, December 31, current year (Lines 36 + 54) (Page 3, Line 38)

Property and Casualty – Assets

See Life Accident and Health – Assets above, it is the same as Property and Casualty – Assets.

Property and Casualty – Liabilities

01 Losses (Part 2A, Line 35, Column 8)
02 Reinsurance payable on paid losses and loss adjustment expenses (Schedule F, Part 1, Column 6)
03 Loss adjustment expenses (Part 2A, Line 35, Column 9)
04 Commissions payable, contingent commissions and other similar charges
05 Other expenses (excluding taxes, licenses and fees)
06 Taxes, licenses and fees (excluding federal and foreign income taxes)
07.1 Current federal and foreign income taxes (including $... on realized capital gains (losses))
07.2 Net deferred tax liability
08 Borrowed money $... and interest thereon $...
09 Unearned premiums (Part 1A, Line 38, Column 5)(after deducting unearned premiums for ceded reinsurance of $ ... and including warranty reserves of $ ... and accrued accident and health experience rating refunds including $... for medical loss ratio rebate per the Public Health Service Act)
10 Advance premium
11.1 Dividends declared and unpaid: Stockholders
11.2 Dividends declared and unpaid: Policyholders
12 Ceded reinsurance premiums payable (net of ceding commissions)

13   Funds held by company under reinsurance treaties (Schedule F, Part 3, Column 19)
14   Amounts withheld or retained by company for account of others
15   Remittances and items not allocated
16   Provision for reinsurance (including $... certified) (Schedule F, Part 8)
17   Net adjustments in assets and liabilities due to foreign exchange rates
18   Drafts outstanding
19   Payable to parent, subsidiaries and affiliates
20   Derivatives
21   Payable for securities
22   Payable for securities lending
23   Liability for amounts held under uninsured plans
24   Capital Notes $... and interest thereon $...
25   Aggregate write-ins for liabilities
26   Total liabilities excluding protected cell liabilities (Lines 1 through 25)
27   Protected cell liabilities
28   Total liabilities (Lines 26 and 27)
29   Aggregate write-ins for special surplus funds
30   Common capital stock
31   Preferred capital stock
32   Aggregate write-ins for other than special surplus
33   Surplus Notes
34   Gross paid in and contributed surplus
35   Unassigned funds (surplus)
36.1   Less treasury stock, at cost: ... shares common (value included in Line 30 $ ...)
36.2   Less treasury stock, at cost: ... shares preferred (value included in Line 31 $ ...)
37   Surplus as regards policyholders (Lines 29 to 35, less 36)(Page 4, Line 39)
38   TOTALS (Page 2, Line 28, Col. 3)

Property and Casualty – Statement of Income

01   Premiums earned (Part 1, Line 35, Column 4)
02   Losses incurred (Part 2, Line 35, Column 7)
03   Loss adjustment expenses incurred (Part 3, Line 25, Column 1)
04   Other underwriting expenses incurred (Part 3, Line 25, Column 2)
05   Aggregate write-ins for underwriting deductions
06   Total underwriting deductions (Lines 2 through 5)
07   Net income of protected cells
08   Net underwriting gain or (loss) (Line 1 minus Line 6 plus Line 7)
09   Net investment income earned (Exhibit of Net Investment Income, Line 17)
10   Net realized capital gains or (losses) less capital gains tax of $... (Exhibit of Capital Gains (Losses))
11   Net investment gain or (loss) (Lines 9 + 10)
12   Net gain (loss) from agents' or premium balances charged off (amount recovered $ ... amount charged off $ ...)
13   Finance and service charges not included in premiums

14 Aggregate write-ins for miscellaneous income
15 Total other income (Lines 12 through 14)
16 Net income before dividends to policyholders, after capital gains tax and before all other federal and foreign income taxes (Lines 8 + 11 + 15)
17 Dividends to policyholders
18 Net income, after dividends to policyholders, after capital gains tax and before all other federal and foreign income taxes (Line 16 minus Line 17)
19 Federal and foreign income taxes incurred
20 Net income (Line 18 minus Line 19)(to Line 22)
21 Surplus as regards policyholders, December 31 prior year (Page 4, Line 39, Column 2)
22 Net income (from Line 20)
23 Net transfers (to) from Protected Cell accounts
24 Change in net unrealized capital gains or (losses) less capital gains tax of $...
25 Change in net unrealized foreign exchange capital gain (loss)
26 Change in net deferred income tax
27 Change in nonadmitted assets (Exhibit of Nonadmitted Assets, Line 26, Column 3)
28 Change in provision for reinsurance (Page 3, Line 16, Column 2 minus Column 1)
29 Change in surplus notes
30 Surplus (contributed to) withdrawn from protected cells
31 Cumulative effect of changes in accounting principles
32.1 Capital changes: Paid in
32.2 Capital changes: Transferred from surplus (Stock Dividend)
32.3 Capital changes: Transferred to surplus
33.1 Surplus adjustments: Paid in
33.2 Surplus adjustments: Transferred to capital (Stock Dividend)
33.3 Surplus adjustments: Transferred from capital
34 Net remittances from or (to) Home Office
35 Dividends to stockholders
36 Change in treasury stock (Page 3, Lines 36.1 and 36.2, Column 2 minus Column 1)
37 Aggregate write-ins for gains and losses in surplus
38 Change in surplus as regards policyholders (Lines 22 through 37)
39 Surplus as regards policyholders, December 31 current year (Lines 21 plus Line 38) (Page 3, Line 37)

Lines of Business in Annual Statement

LAH − Industrial Life, Ordinary Life, Ordinary Individual Annuities, Ordinary Supplementary Contracts, Credit Life (Grp and Indiv), Group Life, Group Annuity, Group Accident and Health, Credit A&H, Other A&H.

PC − Fire, Allied Lines, Farmowners multiple peril, Homeowners multiple peril, Commercial multiple peril, Ocean marine, Inland marine, Financial guaranty, Medical professional liability – occurrence, Medical professional liability - claims-made, Earthquake, Group accident and health, Credit accident and health (group and individual), Other accident and health, Workers' compensation, Other liability – occurrence, Other liability - claims-made, Excess workers' compensation, Products liability – occurrence, Products liability - claims-made, Private passenger auto liability, Commercial auto liability, Auto physical damage, Aircraft (all perils), Fidelity, Surety, Burglary and theft, Boiler and machinery, Credit, International, Warranty.

Basic Accounting

This chapter is designed to give accountants and bookkeepers that are not CPAs the background they need to fully understand and master their accounting duties and qualify them for advancements and promotions. This book will help you understand how to record (journalize) transactions and then create financial statements.

Have you ever thought about the physical law which states that to every action there is always an equal and opposite reaction? When you drop a ball, some of the kinetic energy of the ball is transferred to the floor and also used to flex the material in the ball. The remainder of the energy is retained in the ball and it bounces back up but not quite as high. The difference between the starting height and the ending height represents the energy transferred to the floor and flexing motion.

The same is true with double entry bookkeeping. To every action there is always an equal and opposite reaction so to speak. For instance, if I buy an annual insurance policy, my Prepaid Insurance goes up and my Cash goes down by the same amount. Every month we create an adjusting journal entry to record the prepaid insurance going down by one month's worth of insurance and the insurance expense going up by the same amount.

The Basic Accounting Equation

Assets = Liabilities + Owners Equity + Income – Expense

Practice writing this formula down several times in shorthand such as:

A = L + OE + Inc – Exp

Because Income minus Expenses equals Net Income, we could also write the formula like this:

Assets = Liabilities + Owners Equity + Net Income

Or in shorthand:

A = L + OE + NI

This is essentially what all financial statements are showing. The Balance Sheet has an Assets page and a Liabilities page. The Liabilities page has a Liabilities and Owners Equity or Retained Earning section (they both mean the same thing). The Owners Equity section will always have the Net Income added in to the beginning OE to come up with the ending OE. So the Balance sheet is showing that the Assets equal the Liabilities plus the Ending Owners Equity which includes the Net Income. The Net Income comes from the Income Statement. The Income Statement has an Income page and an Expenses page. The Expenses are subtracted from the Income to come up with the Net Income. If the Net Income is negative, that means the Expenses were greater than the Income so we have a Net Loss from operations.

Let us look at a simple set of financial statements to illustrate this concept.

Assets			
Cash			$75.00
Bonds			150.00
Prepaid Insurance			25.00
Equipment		80.00	
Accumulated Depreciation		-5.00	75.00
Total Assets			**$325.00**

Liabilities		
Accounts Payable		$80.00
Loans Payable		70.00
Total Liablilities		$150.00
Owners Equity		
Beginning OE		$140.00
Net Income		35.00
Ending OE		$175.00
Total Liablities and OE		$325.00

Income

	Sales Revenue	$175.00
	Interest Income	15.00
Total Income		$190.00

Total Expenses		155.00
Net Income (Loss)		$35.00

Expenses

	Salaries	$121.00
	Auto Expense	17.00
	Insurance Expense	5.00
	Interest Expense	4.00
	Advertising	3.00
	Depreciation Expense	5.00
Total Expenses		$155.00

Why do Debits (Dr) always equal Credits (Cr)?

We can rearrange the Basic Accounting Equation by adding Expense to each side to come up with:

Assets + Expense = Liabilities + Owners Equity + Income − Expense + Expense

Which is the same as:

Assets + Expense = Liabilities + Owners Equity + Income

Or

A + Exp = L + OE + Inc

Practice writing down these equations several times also because this is why debits always equal credits!

Debits always equal Credits because...

Debits increase this side of the formula Assets + Expenses, and

Credits increase this side of the formula Liabilities + Owners Equity + Income.

More completely, Dr Increase and Cr Decrease this side of the formula A + Exp

And, Cr Increase and Dr Decrease this side of the formula L + OE + Inc

You can write this formula on two lines like this:

    Assets + Expenses   =   Liabilities + Owners Equity + Income

      Dr +, Cr -   Cr +, Dr –

So,   Dr Increase this side and   Cr Increase this side

And Cr Decrease this side and   Dr Decrease this side

Practice writing this two line equation several times.

How to Journalize Transactions

Using the formula discussed above:

    Assets + Expenses   =   Liabilities + Owners Equity + Income

      Dr +, Cr -   Cr +, Dr –

Let us run through some examples of different transactions

	Debit	**Credit**
Asset		
Prepaid Insurance (A+)	30.00	

Cash in Bank (A-) 30.00

To record purchase of Annual Insurance Policy.

Equipment (A+) 80.00
    Loan Payable (L+) 80.00

To record purchase of equipment with proceeds from Loan.

Depreciation Expense (Exp+) 5.00
    Accumulated Depreciation (A-) 5.00

To record periodic depreciation.

Liability

Interest Expense (Exp+) 4.00
Loan Payable (L-) 10.00
    Cash (A-) 14.00

To record monthly loan payment, part of which is interest.

Expense

Automobile Expense (Exp+) 17.00
    Cash in Bank (A-) 17.00

To record cash paid to gas station.

Insurance Expense (Exp+)	5.00	
Prepaid Insurance (A-)		5.00

To charge off prepaid insurance for time passed.

Income

Cash in Bank (A+)	175	
Sales Revenue (Inc+)		175

To record Sale of Merchandise

Investment Accounting

Bonds

First, let's look at a general overview of bonds and then we can discuss how to record typical transactions. Bonds are promises to pay a face value, the par value, at a specified maturity date in the future. Typically a bond will pay interest every six months at a stated rate of interest, also called the coupon rate. The stated rate of interest is expressed as an annual rate. If a bond pays 6% on a semiannual basis and the par value is 100,000 you will receive 3,000 every 6 months which equals 100,000 * .06 / 2. So the 3,000 interest payment equals the Face Value of 100,000 times the annual interest rate of 6% divided by the number of payments per year which is 2 for a semiannual bond. If this was a monthly bond then the monthly interest amount would equal

500 = 100,000 * .06 / 12 since there are 12 payments every year.

Bonds are not usually purchased at face value. In other words, if we are buying a 100,000 bond we do not typically pay 100,000. The reason we do not pay face value for a bond is that the interest rate it pays is not typically the same as the market rate of interest at the purchase date.

Let's say the market rate of interest is actually 7%. So we could buy a 7% bond at par. We would probably buy a 6% bond for less than par so that it yields closer to the market rate. Buying a bond for less than par is said to be buying a bond at a *Discount*. If the market rate was 5% then we would pay more than the face value of a 6% bond which is said to be buying the bond at a *Premium*.

The difference between our purchase price and the par value charged off to the Income Statement over the life of the bond such that the Interest plus or minus the Amortization will net to earnings being recognized for the bond at approximately the market rate. Specifically, when we buy a bond at a premium or discount, we can calculate the exact yield we will be earning on the bond. That yield is called the *Effective Rate*.

If we bought the bond at a Premium then the Book Value (purchase cost) will be greater than the Par Value. This excess debit sitting in the Asset account needs to be charged off to the Income Statement periodically as Amortization of Premium. *Premium amortization is a Debit* to the income statement and represents an expense. Interest income is a credit to the income statement. If we net the Premium amortization debit with the Interest income credit we get actual earnings credit from the bond at less than the interest rate.

If we bought the bond at a Discount then the Book Value (purchase cost) will be less than the Par Value. This shortage needs to be charged off to the Income Statement periodically as Amortization of Discount so that at maturity the Book Value will be equal to the Par Value. *Discount amortization is a Credit* to the income statement and represents income. Interest income is a credit to the income statement. If we combine the Discount amortization credit with the Interest income credit we get actual earnings credit from the bond at greater than the interest rate.

This is how we amortize a bond…

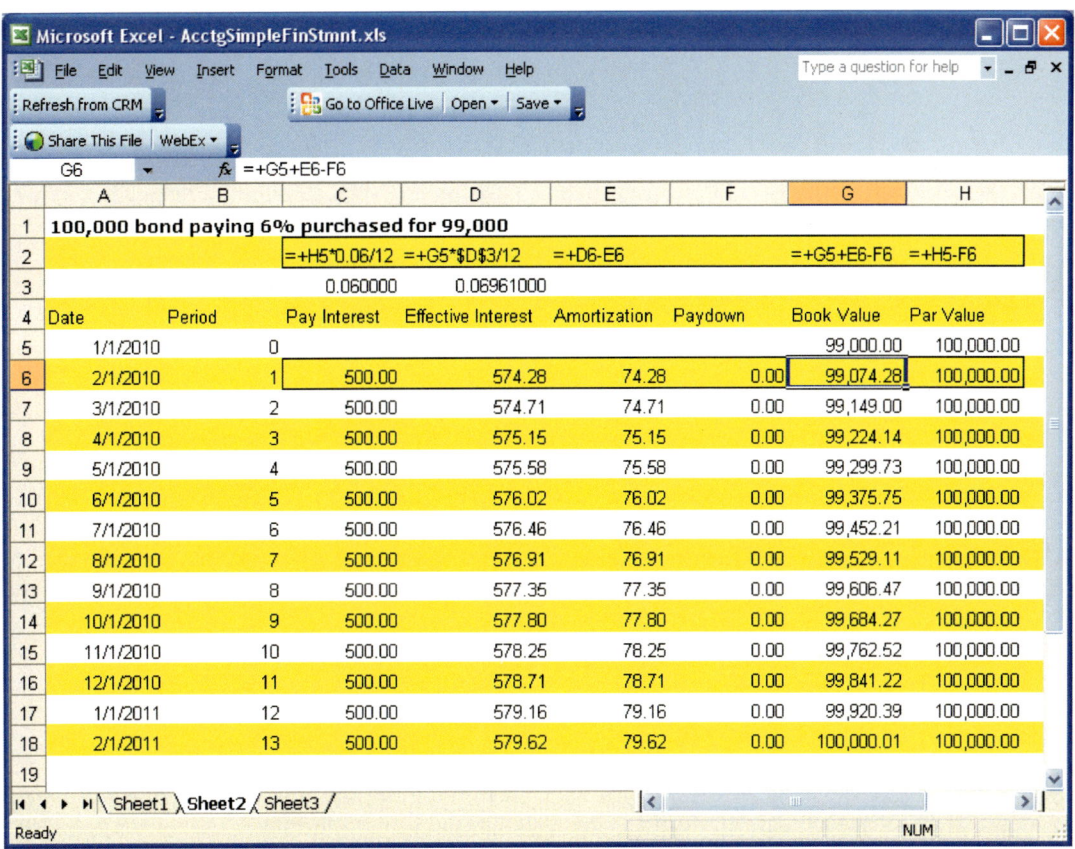

Notice the formulas for line 6 are detailed in line 2. Basically you take the Par times the annual stated rate divided by the number of periods per year in column C. This is the interest you will receive. Then you take the Book Value times the annual effective rate divided by the periods per year in column D. This is the actual earnings for the bond. The difference between those two amounts is amortization and it is added to the beginning Book Value to equal the ending Book Value then it starts all over again for the next period. So the effective rate of 6.961% will amortize the bond purchased 1/1/2010 for 99,000 up to 100,000 at the maturity date of Feb 1, 2011.

Solving for the effective rate is an iterative process. You will need to try this two or three times before you find the exact effective rate so that Book = Par at the maturity date. What you do is first take a guess at the effective rate to get close and then see how much you are off at the maturity date. For instance in the above example, if we first put in .067, the ending book value will be 99,709.20 which is different from the par of 100,000 by 290.80. If we change the effective rate to .069 the book value ends up at 99,931.97. So, if a .002 change in the effective rate moves the book value at maturity date by 222.77 = 99,931.97 – 99,709.20 how much of a change to the effective rate will move the book value by our difference, 290.80?

The way you solve this is by using a proration formula like this

.002 / 222.77 is proportional to X / 290.80

You read this like so: .002 is to 222.77 as X is to 290.80.

To solve a proportion, you cross multiply and solve for X.

.002	Proportional to	X
222.77		290.80

So,   222.77 * X = .002 * 290.80

Or,   222.77 * X = .5816

X = .5816 / 222.77 (divide both sides by 222.77 to get rid of it on the left side)

X = 0.0026107644655923149436638685639898

Then we add this number to our original .067 to equal .0696107644656.

If we use that number as the effective rate in the amortization table the book value ends up as 100,000.09 at the maturity date a difference of 9 cents. The reason it is not exact is because this is a geometric function, not a straight line function. You would have to solve the formula again like this to get an exact 100,000.00 book value at maturity date….

If a difference of .00061076446 moves the book value by 68.12 = 99931.97 – 100000.09 then how much change to the effective rate would move the book value by 68.03?

Now that we know more about bonds and how to journalize basic transactions, let us look at how we would record some typical bond transactions.

	Debit	**Credit**
Bond (A+)	95,000	
Cash in Bank		95,000

Record purchase of bond.

	Debit	**Credit**
Bond (A+)	50	
Discount Amortization (Inc+)		50

Record periodic amortization of discount.

	Debit	**Credit**
Cash in Bank (A+)	1,200	
Discount Amortization (Inc+)		50
Bond (A net -)	50	1,000
Interest Income (Inc+)		200

To record monthly interest of 200, monthly amortization of 50 and mortgage paydown of 1,000. Notice the net credit to the income statement is $250 although the bond only pays $200.

	Debit	**Credit**
Bond	25	
Interest Receivable	100	
Discount Amortization		25
Interest Income		100

To record Accrued Interest and Amortization for the end of the month to recognize half a month's worth of interest and amortization since the bond pays on the 15th every month.

	Debit	**Credit**
Cash in Bank (A+)	100,200	
Interest Income (Inc+)		200
Discount Amortization (Inc+)		50
Bond (A net -)	50	100,000

To record Maturity of Bond along with final interest payment and final Amortization adjustment.

	Debit	**Credit**
Cash in Bank (A+)	94,000	
Realized Loss (Exp+)	225	
Bond (A-)		94,100
Interest Income (Inc+)		125

To record Sale of Bond for $94,000 cash which includes $125 of interest income.

The Sale transaction illustrates a formula you should memorize to record bond sales.

Total Cash from Sale including interest is	94,000
Minus Interest of	125
Equals Consideration of	93,875
Less Book Value of	94,100
Equals Gain (Loss)	(225)

Partial Sales and Calls

You should recognize interest income and amortization up to the settlement date of the sale or call. This can be done by prorating between scheduled payment dates on the amortization schedule. For instance if the settlement date of the sale is 90 days from the last semiannual payment, you can take 90/180 of the next scheduled payment amounts for interest and amortization times the par value sold ratio to determine the interest and amortization to record on the sale transaction. By doing this, you will have the correct Interest and Book Value to subtract from the Total Cash so that the Realized gain or loss is correct. You will also need to adjust the amortization schedule to show the partial sale/call inserted into the schedule and the reduced amount of par value going forward in future periods. See formula for calculating Gain (Loss) above.

Permanent Declines

If a bonds value has substantially declined because of credit risk and there is little likelihood that the value will improve, a permanent decline will write down the Book Value and the Cost Basis to the Market or Fair value. You would not write down the Tax Basis though. This write down is recorded as a debit to Realized Loss (Exp +) and a credit to Book Value (A-). The realized loss is reported in the Other Than Temporary Impairments column on D part 1.

Mortgage Backed Bonds

Mortgage backed bonds pay you some principal along with the interest each month. When you make your mortgage payment on your home part of your payment is interest and part is principal. It is the same with mortgage backed bonds. The issuer passes along the return of principal to the bond holder each month. When an underlying mortgage defaults, if the mortgage is secured, then the bond holder can receive the foreclosed amount also which effectively accelerates the return of principal. The rate of prepayment is sometimes published as a PSA or CPR factor which can be used to project a repayment stream on the amortization schedule. First, let's talk about a mortgage backed bond without the PSA and CPR factors.

When you purchase a mortgage backed bond the amortization schedule is computed using a specific effective interest rate. When the paydowns come in, you need to recognize some additional amortization equal to the present value of the future amortization you would have recognized had you held that par value. Or, stated another way, if you knew when you bought the bond that you were going to receive this par value, how much additional amortization would you have already recognized to record this par value being redeemed. Either way, recognizing additional amortization so that you can hold the effective rate constant so that the Book Value will still equal the Par Value at maturity date is called the "Retrospective Method". Alternatively, you could change the effective rate on the amortization schedule which would spread the additional amortization over the remaining life which is called the "Prospective Method". Practically though everyone uses the Retrospective Method. The Retrospective Method is recommended by auditors.

If you are using PSA factors to project a serial repayment stream on a bond then you should use the Prospective Method, change the effective rate, to record the paydowns. The Prospective method will result in a consistent amortization amount being recognized. The Retrospective method, holding the effective rate constant is not valid since the repayment stream is constantly changing everytime a payment comes in and everytime a new PSA factor is applied. Usually the new PSA factors are imported quarterly.

Stepped Bonds

Stepped bonds will vary the rate of interest that they are going to pay you over the life of the bond. This makes for an interesting amortization schedule! If a bond pays a below market rate at the beginning, like 2% then 4% then an above market rate at the end like 6% then 8% for instance, the effective interest rate might be 5% for the life of the bond. In this case, the amortization schedule will show discount amortization in the beginning and premium amortization at the end.

Many times you will not want to record all the stepped rates in the amortization schedule because while technically correct, practically it yields strange results. Frequently the bonds start out paying low interest rates and then much higher rates in the future. This usually results in recognizing discount amortization to increase the book value amount much higher than the par value amount in the early years. The problem comes in when you then sell the bond and have to record a large loss to offset the large discount amortization which was recognized earlier. Even though your bosses may argue that amortizing a bond using the stepped rates is correct, they will not like to see the large loss that results from being correct. You should argue that the principal of Amortizing to Worst should be applied in this situation.

Amortizing to Worst is generally applied to Premium bonds that have call dates earlier than the Maturity date. By amortizing to the earlier call date the recognition of Premium amortization (an expense) is accelerated which is a more conservative approach. Similarly in a Stepped bond situation, recognizing a lot more Discount amortization (income) by being technically correct is not a conservative approach.

Treasury Inflation Protected Bonds (TIPS)

TIPS bonds vary the amount of Par they will be paying based on an inflation index. If inflation goes up then the amount of par you own will go up as well. When the par value goes up you will now be amortizing to this new par value. The par can go down also! The NAIC wants you to report the Fair Value of the bond in the Carrying Value column. So, TIPS bonds will necessarily have an Unrealized amount reported on D1 and also an amortization amount. The change in the Fair Value for the year net of the amortization is what is shown in the Unrealized column. As if that was not enough, the NAIC would also like you to report the Original Issued Par Value for the bond in the Par Value column, not the par you currently own for TIPS bonds.

Technically, the correct Statutory approach for TIPs bonds is to keep amortizing to the Par Value that you originally purchased. This will result in less amortization and more unrealized gain on the D reports if the Par value increases. The Gaap approach of adjusting the amortization schedule to the new Par value and amortizing to the new Par value is easier for accounting purposes. The Fair Value rates are all applied to the current Par values and when sales occur, you will need to sell the correct percentage of the current Par values. Accountants can end up making complicated mistakes if the Par value on the TIPS bonds is not kept current.

Valuation of Bonds for the Annual Statement

There is a Carrying Value column on Schedule D part 1 of the annual statement which is usually the Book Value, also known as the Amortized Cost. However, depending on the NAIC Designation, the Carrying Value might be the Lower of Book Value or Fair Value. These rules depend on the type of insurance company. For Life companies, if a bond is classified with an NAIC Designation of 6 then you must enter the lower of fair value or amortized cost. For Property and Casualty and Health companies, if a bond is classified with an NAIC Designation of 3, 4, 5 or 6 then you must enter the lower of fair value or amortized cost. The Securities Valuation Office has published a cross reference between the Moody's and S&P Ratings and the NAIC Designations, see below.

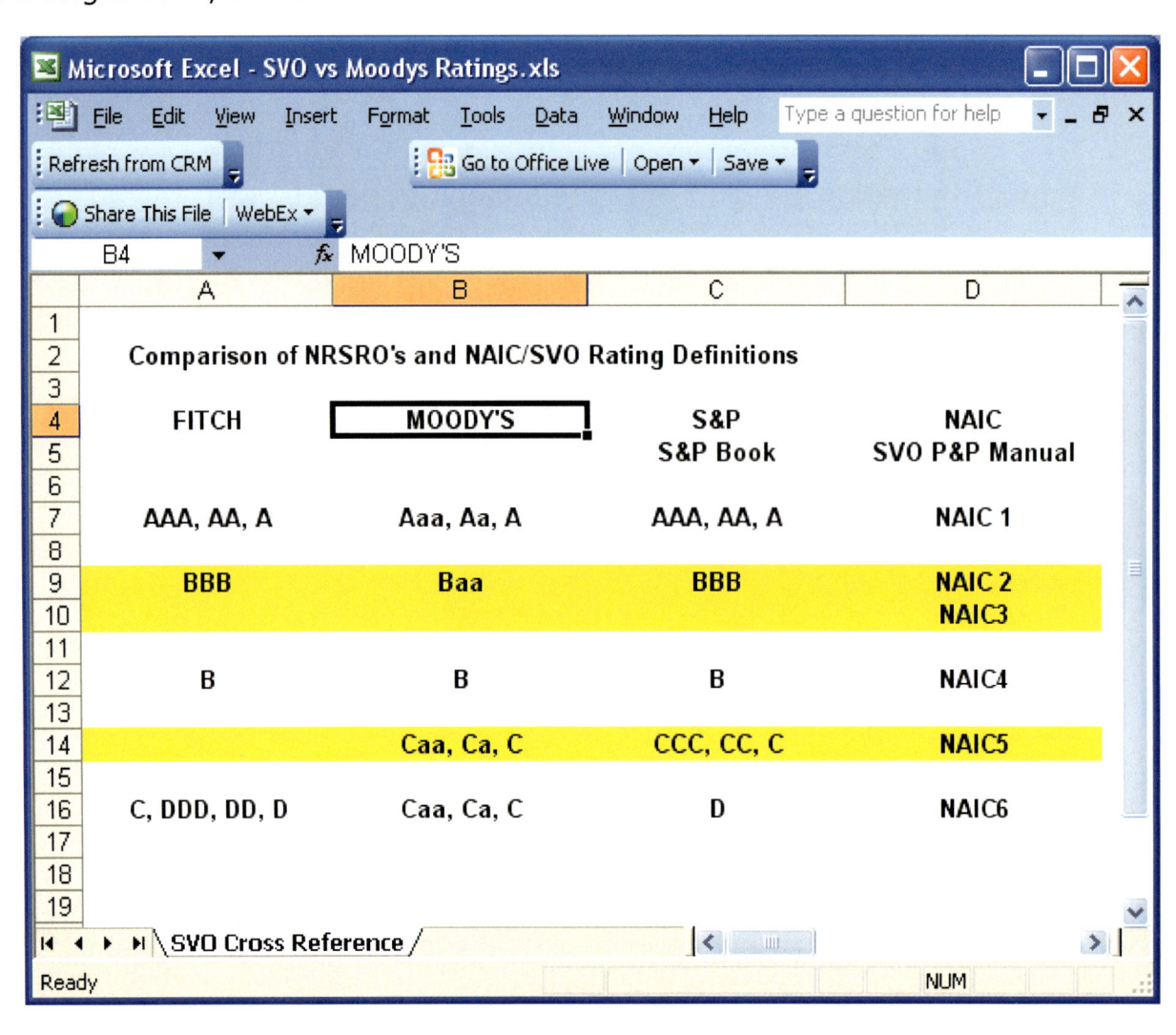

Comparison of NRSRO's and NAIC/SVO Rating Definitions

FITCH	MOODY'S	S&P / S&P Book	NAIC SVO P&P Manual
AAA, AA, A	Aaa, Aa, A	AAA, AA, A	NAIC 1
BBB	Baa	BBB	NAIC 2
			NAIC3
B	B	B	NAIC4
	Caa, Ca, C	CCC, CC, C	NAIC5
C, DDD, DD, D	Caa, Ca, C	D	NAIC6

When a bond is reporting the Fair Value amount in the Carrying Value column on Schedule D part 1, there will typically be an unrealized gain or loss amount reported as well. Some people mistakenly assume the Unrealized column should report the life to date unrealized adjustment recognized on the bond but this is not always the case. Keep in mind when creating the Verification Between Periods (DVER) schedule you are explaining the difference between the beginning of the year and the end of the year carrying value amounts. The Unrealized column amounts are part of that formula.

The DVER is replicated here to help you understand the situation, see below. Notice the Unrealized coming in from Schedule D Part 1 on line 4.1. Basically, the DVER proves the following (Simplified by intent) formula to be true taking amounts from the Schedule D reports.

Beginning Book/Carrying Value plus Purchases plus Amortization plus Unrealized minus Realized Loss from Permanent Declines minus Book Value Sold equals Ending Book Value.

Actually, the DVER does not subtract the Book Value Sold, it grosses that up by subtracting the Consideration on the Sale adding back the Realized Gain on the Sale and subtracting out the Realized Loss on the Sale which equals the Book Value Sold. Additionally, it does not just add the amortization; it adds the discount amortization and subtracts the premium amortization.

Schedule D - Verification - Bonds and Stock

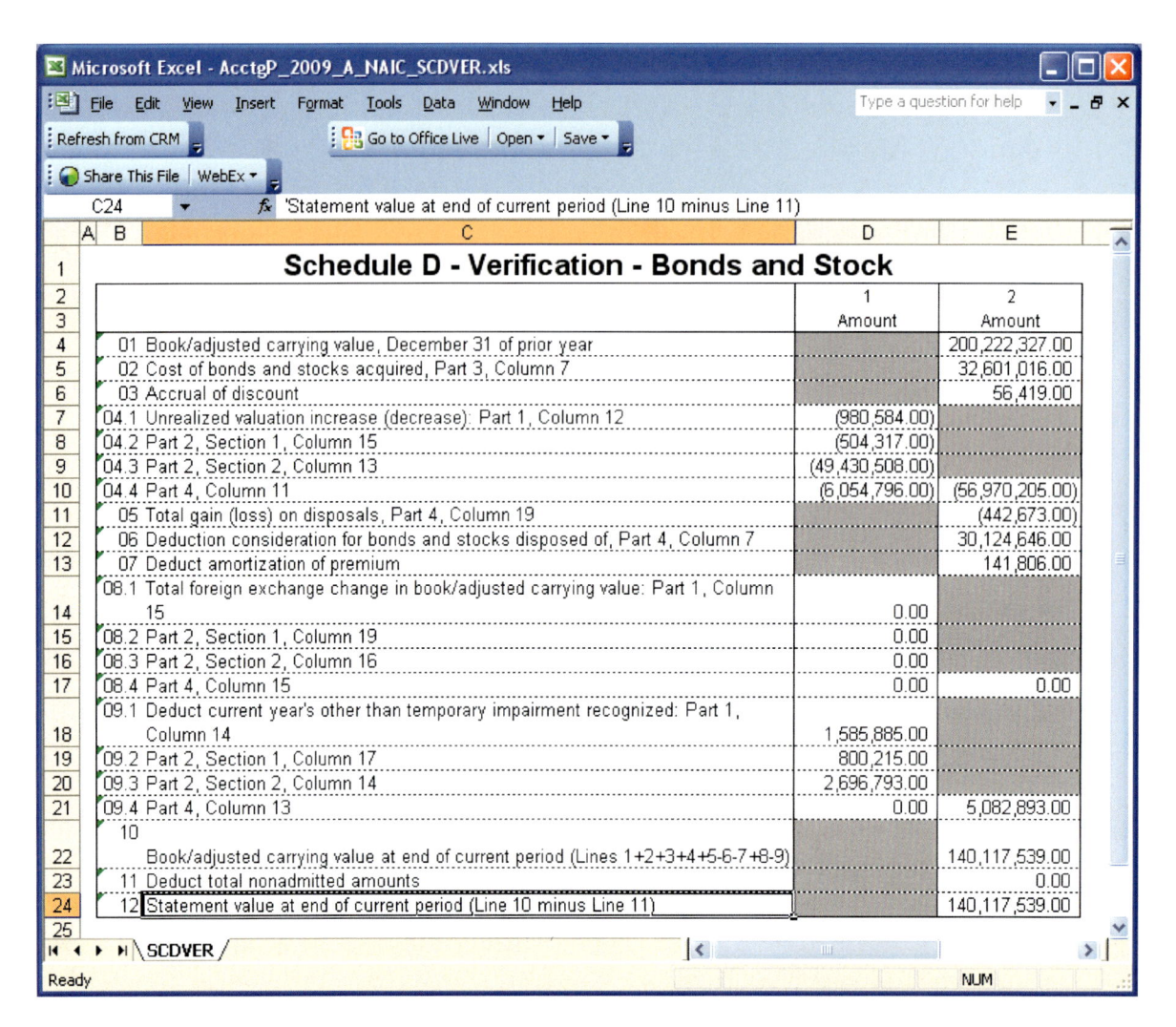

		1 Amount	2 Amount
01	Book/adjusted carrying value, December 31 of prior year		200,222,327.00
02	Cost of bonds and stocks acquired, Part 3, Column 7		32,601,016.00
03	Accrual of discount		56,419.00
04.1	Unrealized valuation increase (decrease): Part 1, Column 12	(980,584.00)	
04.2	Part 2, Section 1, Column 15	(504,317.00)	
04.3	Part 2, Section 2, Column 13	(49,430,508.00)	
04.4	Part 4, Column 11	(6,054,796.00)	(56,970,205.00)
05	Total gain (loss) on disposals, Part 4, Column 19		(442,673.00)
06	Deduction consideration for bonds and stocks disposed of, Part 4, Column 7		30,124,646.00
07	Deduct amortization of premium		141,806.00
08.1	Total foreign exchange change in book/adjusted carrying value: Part 1, Column 15	0.00	
08.2	Part 2, Section 1, Column 19	0.00	
08.3	Part 2, Section 2, Column 16	0.00	
08.4	Part 4, Column 15	0.00	0.00
09.1	Deduct current year's other than temporary impairment recognized: Part 1, Column 14	1,585,885.00	
09.2	Part 2, Section 1, Column 17	800,215.00	
09.3	Part 2, Section 2, Column 14	2,696,793.00	
09.4	Part 4, Column 13	0.00	5,082,893.00
10	Book/adjusted carrying value at end of current period (Lines 1+2+3+4+5-6-7+8-9)		140,117,539.00
11	Deduct total nonadmitted amounts		0.00
12	Statement value at end of current period (Line 10 minus Line 11)		140,117,539.00

If the bond was valued at Fair Value for both the beginning and end of the period then the unrealized columns will equal the current year Fair Value minus the prior year fair value minus the current year amortization. In other words because they also need to report the amortization, it must be netted into the total fair value change.

If the bond was valued at Book Value for the beginning of the year and Fair Value at the end of the year the unrealized column will equal the current year fair value minus the current year amortized cost.

If the bond was valued at Fair Value for the beginning of the year and Book Value at the end of the year the unrealized column will equal the prior year amortized cost minus the prior year fair value.

	Debit	**Credit**

Stocks

Stocks (A+)	75,000	
Cash in Bank (A-)		75000

To record Stock Purchase

Cash in Bank (A+)	38	
Dividend Income (Inc+)		38

To record dividend income received

Fair Value Increase (A+)	375	
Unrealized Gain (OE+)		375

To record Fair Value Adjustment

Cash in Bank	25	
Stocks		25

To record Liquidating Dividend as return of cost basis

Stock Split – No adjustment necessary to dollar balances. Only need to adjust the total number of shares and the per share amounts.

Useful Formulas and Excel Techniques for Accountants

Being able to sort a block of data by Account Number for instance and then write a formula to automatically subtotal it can be useful if you have a large set of data. The way you solve this problem is to break it up into a few smaller formulas. First you need an indicator column to test for when the account number changes. I like to put a 1 on the first new account number row and 0 on all the other rows. The formula in C4 below says if A4 is the same as the previous account number A3 then put a 0 otherwise put a 1. So we get a 1 on the first row of each new account number set. The formula in D4 says if C4 = 1 then we are starting a new account number set so add just B4 otherwise add B4 plus D3 which would be the running total of this account number set. The formula in E4 says if C5 = 1 then the next row is a new account number set so report D4, the running total of this current account number set otherwise enter a blank.

	A	B	C	D	E
1					
2			=IF(A4=A3,0,1)	=IF(C4=1,+B4,+B4+D3)	=IF(C5=1,+D4,"")
3	Account Number	Amount	Change Indicator	Accumulated	Account Total
4	123-AB-00	316.71	1	316.71	
5	123-AB-00	21.29	0	338.00	
6	123-AB-00	4,375.00	0	4,713.00	
7	123-AB-00	2,126.52	0	6,839.52	6,839.52
8	123-AB-10	1,811.48	1	1,811.48	
9	123-AB-10	2,153.33	0	3,964.81	
10	123-AB-10	1,345.83	0	5,310.64	5,310.64
11	223-AB-00	1,345.83	1	1,345.83	
12	223-AB-00	242.07	0	1,587.90	
13	223-AB-00	1,694.47	0	3,282.37	
14	223-AB-00	363.10	0	3,645.47	
15	223-AB-00	1,331.37	0	4,976.84	4,976.84
16	323-AB-00	11,250.00	1	11,250.00	11,250.00
17	423-AB-00	2,062.45	1	2,062.45	2,062.45
18	523-AB-00	1,443.71	1	1,443.71	1,443.71
19	623-AB-00	1,546.84	1	1,546.84	
20	623-AB-00	3,873.00	0	5,419.84	
21	623-AB-00	2,344.00	0	7,763.84	7,763.84
22	723-AB-00	3,854.00	1	3,854.00	
23	723-AB-00	7,875.00	0	11,729.00	
24	723-AB-00	8,333.00	0	20,062.00	
25	723-AB-00	1,756.25	0	21,818.25	21,818.25
26			1		
27		61,465.25			61,465.25

Solving a Proration Formula

As discussed in the Bond effective interest rate section, solving a proportion is one of the most useful equations for accountants. Let us look at another example. Consider two lots of the same bond, Bond A has 77,234 of par and Bond B has 52,978 of par. If bond A received $573.25 of interest for the month, how much interest did bond B receive assuming they both pay the same interest rate?

The way you solve this is by using a proration formula like this

573.25 / 77,234 is proportional to X / 52,978

You read this like so: 573.25 is to 77,234 as X is to 52,978.

To solve a proportion, you cross multiply and solve for X.

$$\frac{573.25}{77,234} \quad \text{Proportional to} \quad \frac{X}{52,978}$$

So, 77,234 * X = 573.25 * 52,978

Or, 77,234 * X = 30,369,638.5

X = 30,369,638.5 / 77,234 (divide both sides by 77,234 to get rid of it on the left)

X = 393.22

So the 52,978 par value bond should have received 393.22 of interest.

Appendix A

Life Accident and Health

Cover Page
Jurat Page
Assets
Liabilities, Surplus and Other Funds
Summary of Operations
Cash Flow
Analysis of Operations by Lines of Business
Analysis of Increase in Reserves During the Year
Exhibit of Net Investment Income
Exhibit of Capital Gains (Losses)
Exhibit 1 Part 1 - Premiums and Annuity Considerations
Exhibit 1 Part 2 - Dividends and Coupons Applied
Exhibit 2 - General Expenses
Exhibit 3 - Taxes, Licenses and Fees
Exhibit 4 - Dividends or Refunds
Exhibit 5 - Aggregate Reserve for Life Contracts
Exhibit 5 - Interrogatories
Exhibit 5A - Changes in Bases of Valuation During the Year
Exhibit 6 - Aggregate Reserves for Accident and Health Contracts
Exhibit 7 - Deposit-Type Contracts
Exhibit 8 - Contract Claims - Part 1 - Liability End of Current Year
Exhibit 8 - Contract Claims - Part 2 - Incurred During the Year
Exhibit of Nonadmitted Assets
Notes to Financial Statements
General Interrogatories - Part 1 - General
General Interrogatories - Part 1 - Board of Directors
General Interrogatories - Part 1 - Financial
General Interrogatories - Part 1 - Investment
General Interrogatories - Part 1 - Other
General Interrogatories - Part 2
Five Year Historical Data
Direct Business - Part 1
Direct Business - Part 2
Direct Business - Part 3
Exhibit of Life Insurance
Exhibit of Life Insurance - Part 2
Exhibit of Life Insurance - Part 3
Exhibit of Life Insurance - Part 4
Exhibit of Life Insurance - Part 5

Exhibit of Life Insurance - Part 6
Exhibit of Life Insurance - Part 7
Exhibit of Life Insurance - Policies with Disability Provisions
Exhibit of Number of Policies, Contracts, ...Supplementary Contracts
Exhibit of Number of Policies, Contracts, ...Annuities
Exhibit of Number of Policies, Contracts, ...Accident and Health Insurance
Exhibit of Number of Policies, Contracts, ...Deposit Funds
Interest Maintenance Reserve
Interest Maintenance Reserve - Amortization
Asset Valuation Reserve
Asset Valuation Reserve - Default Component
Asset Valuation Reserve - Equity Component
Asset Valuation Reserve Replications (Synthetic) Assets
Schedule F - Claims
Schedule H - Part 1 - Analysis of Underwriting Operations
Schedule H - Part 2 - Reserves and Liabilities
Schedule H - Part 3 - Prior Year's Claim Reserves and Liabilities
Schedule H - Part 4 - Reinsurance
Schedule H - Part 5 - Health Claims
Schedule S - Part 1 - Section 1
Schedule S - Part 1 - Section 2
Schedule S - Part 2
Schedule S - Part 3 - Section 1
Schedule S - Part 3 - Section 2
Schedule S - Part 4
Schedule S - Part 4 - Bank Footnote
Schedule S - Part 5
Schedule S - Part 5 - Bank Footnote
Schedule S - Part 6
Schedule S - Part 7
Schedule T - Premiums and Annuity Considerations
Schedule T - Part 2 - Interstate Compact
Schedule Y - Part 1
Schedule Y - Part 1A - Detail of Insurance Holding Company System
Schedule Y - Part 1A - Explanations
Schedule Y - Part 2
Supplemental Exhibits and Schedules Interrogatories
Overflow Page for Write-ins
Summary Investment Schedule
Schedule A - Verification - Real Estate
Schedule B - Verification - Mortgage Loans
Schedule BA - Verification - Other Long-Term Invested Assets
Schedule D - Verification - Bonds and Stock

Schedule D - Summary By Country
Schedule D - Part 1A - Section 1 - Quality and Maturity Distribution of All Bonds Owned by Major Type and NAIC Designation
Schedule D - Part 1A - Section 2 - Quality and Maturity Distribution of All Bonds Owned by Major Type and Subtype
Schedule DA - Verification - Short-Term Investments
Schedule DB - Part A - Verification - Options, Caps, Floors, Collars, Swaps and Forwards
Schedule DB - Part B - Verification - Futures Contracts
Schedule DB - Part C - Section 1 - Replication (Synthetic Asset) Transactions (RSATs) Open
Schedule DB-Part C-Section 2-Reconciliation of Replication (Synthetic Asset) Transactions Open
Schedule DB - Verification - Book/Adjusted Carrying Value, Fair Value and Potential Exposure of Derivatives
Schedule E - Verification - Cash Equivalents
Schedule A - Part 1 - Real Estate Owned
Schedule A - Part 2 - Real Estate Acquired and Additions Made
Schedule A - Part 3 - Real Estate Disposed
Schedule B - Part 1 - Mortgage Loans Owned
Schedule B - Part 2 - Mortgage Loans Acquired and Additions Made
Schedule B - Part 3 - Mortgage Loans Disposed, Transferred or Repaid
Schedule BA - Part 1 - Other Long-Term Invested Assets Owned
Schedule BA - Part 2 - Other Long-Term Invested Assets Acquired and Additions Made
Schedule BA - Part 3 - Other Long-Term Invested Assets Disposed, Transferred or Repaid
Schedule D - Part 1 - Long Term Bonds Owned
Schedule D - Part 2 - Section 1 - Preferred Stocks Owned
Schedule D - Part 2 - Section 2 - Common Stocks Owned
Schedule D - Part 3 - Long-Term Bonds and Stocks Acquired
Schedule D - Part 4 - Long-Term Bonds and Stocks Sold, Redeemed or Otherwise Disposed Of
Schedule D - Part 5 - Long Term Bonds and Stocks Acquired and Fully Disposed Of
Schedule D-Part 6-Section 1-Valuation of Shares of Subsidiary, Controlled or Affiliated Companies
Schedule D - Part 6 - Section 2
Schedule DA - Part 1 - Short-Term Investments Owned
Schedule DB - Part A - Section 1 - Options, Caps, Floors, Collars, Swaps and Forwards Open
Schedule DB - Part A - Section 2 - Options, Caps, Floors, Collars, Swaps and Forwards Terminated
Schedule DB - Part B - Section 1 - Futures Contracts Open
Schedule DB - Part B - Section 1B - Brokers with whom cash deposits have been made
Schedule DB - Part B - Section 2 - Futures Contracts Terminated
Schedule DB - Part D - Section 1 - Counterparty Exposure for Derivative Instruments Open
Schedule DB - Part D-Section 2 - Collateral for Derivative Instruments Open - Pledged By
Schedule DB - Part D-Section 2 - Collateral for Derivative Instruments Open - Pledged To
Schedule DL - Part 1 - Reinvested Collateral Assets Owned
Schedule DL - Part 2 - Reinvested Collateral Assets Owned
Schedule E - Part 1 - Month End Depository Balances
Schedule E - Part 2 - Cash Equivalents Owned

Schedule E - Part 3 - Special Deposits
Accident and Health Policy Experience Exhibit
Accident and Health Policy Experience Exhibit Summary Part 1 - Individual Policies
Accident and Health Policy Experience Exhibit Summary Part 2 - Group Policies
Accident and Health Policy Experience Exhibit Summary Part 3 - Credit Policies (Individual and Group)
Accident and Health Policy Experience Exhibit Summary Part 4 - All Individual, Group and Credit Policies
Supplemental Health Care Exhibit - Part 1
Supplemental Health Care Exhibit - Part 1 - Other Indicators
Supplemental Health Care Exhibit - Part 2
Supplemental Health Care Exhibit - Part 3
Supplemental Health Care Exhibit's Expense Allocation Report - Description of Allocation Methodology
Supplemental Health Care Exhibit's Expense Allocation Report - Desc of Quality Improvement Expenses
Audited Financial Information
Accountant's Letter of Qualifications
Communication of Internal Control Related Matters Noted in Audit
Management's Report of Internal Control Over Financial Reporting
Relief from the five-year rotation requirement for lead audit partner
Relief from the one-year cooling off period for independent CPA
Relief from the Requirements for Audit Committees
Credit Insurance Experience Exhibit Cover
Credit Insurance Experience Exhibit - Part 1A
Credit Insurance Experience Exhibit - Part 1B
Credit Insurance Experience Exhibit - Part 2A
Credit Insurance Experience Exhibit - Part 2B
Credit Insurance Experience Exhibit - Part 2C
Credit Insurance Experience Exhibit - Part 2D
Credit Insurance Experience Exhibit - Part 3A
Credit Insurance Experience Exhibit - Part 3B
Credit Insurance Experience Exhibit - Part 4
Credit Insurance Experience Exhibit - Part 5
Credit Insurance Experience Exhibit - Part 6
Interest Sensitive Life Cover
ISL - Analysis of Operations by Lines of Business
ISL - Interest Sensitive Life - Analysis of Increase in Reserves and Deposit Funds
Interest Sensitive Life Overflow Page for Write-ins
Supplemental Investment Risks Interrogatories
GMR
Adjustments To The GMR
Long-Term Care Experience Reporting Form 1
Long-Term Care Experience Reporting Form 2A - Individual

Long-Term Care Experience Reporting Form 2A - Individual
Long-Term Care Experience Reporting Form 2B - Group
Long-Term Care Experience Reporting Form 2C - Summary
Long-Term Care Experience Reporting Form 3 - Individual - Part 1
Long-Term Care Experience Reporting Form 3 - Individual - Part 2
Long-Term Care Experience Reporting Form 3 - Individual - Part 3
Long-Term Care Experience Reporting Form 3 - Individual - Part 4
Long-Term Care Experience Reporting Form 3 - Group - Part 1
Long-Term Care Experience Reporting Form 3 - Group - Part 2
Long-Term Care Experience Reporting Form 3 - Group - Part 3
Long-Term Care Experience Reporting Form 3 - Group - Part 4
Long-Term Care Experience Reporting Form 3 - Summary - Part 1
Long-Term Care Experience Reporting Form 3 - Summary - Part 2
Long-Term Care Experience Reporting Form 3 - Summary - Part 3
Long-Term Care Experience Reporting Form 3 - Summary - Part 4
Long-Term Care Experience Reporting Form 4
Long-Term Care Experience Reporting Form 5
Management's Discussion and Analysis
Medicare Supplement - State/Policy Form Information
Medicare Part D Coverage Supplement
Non-guaranteed Opinion for Exhibit 5
Participating Opinion for Exhibit 5
Schedule SIS
Schedule SIS II
Schedule SIS III
Schedule SIS IV
Regulatory Asset Adequacy Issues Summary (RAAIS) required by Actuarial Opinion and Memorandum Regulation (Model 822), Se
Actuarial Memorandum Required by Actuarial Guideline XXXVIII 8D
Actuarial Certifications Related to Hedging required by Actuarial Guideline XLIII
Financial Officer Certification Related to Clearly Defined Hedging Strategy required by Actuarial Guideline XLIII
Management Certification That the Valuation Reflects Management's Intent required by Actuarial Guideline XLIII
Actuarial Certification Related to the Reserves required by Actuarial Guideline XLIII
Statement of Actuarial Opinion
Actuarial Opinion on X-Factors
Actuarial Opinion on Separate Accounts Funding Guaranteed Minimum Benefit
Actuarial Opinion on Synthetic Guaranteed Investment Contracts
Reasonableness of Assumptions Certification required by Actuarial Guideline XXXV
Reasonableness and Consistency of Assumptions Certification required by Actuarial Guideline XXXV
Reasonableness of Assumptions Certification for Implied Guaranteed Rate Method required by Actuarial Guideline XXXVI
Reasonableness and Consistency of Assumptions Certification required by Actuarial Guideline XXXVI

(Updated Average Market Value)
Reasonableness and Consistency of Assumptions Certification required by Actuarial Guideline XXXVI (Updated Market Value)
Actuarial Certifications Related to Annuity Nonforfeiture Ongoing Compliance for Equity Indexed Annuities
Modified Guaranteed Annuity Model Regulation
Actuarial Certification Related to the Use of 2001 Preferred Class Tables
Supplemental Compensation Exhibit

Property and Casualty

Cover Page
Jurat Page
Assets
Liabilities, Surplus and Other Funds
Underwriting and Investment Exhibit - Statement of Income
Cash Flow
Underwriting and Investment Exhibit - Part 1 - Premiums Earned
Underwriting and Investment Exhibit - Part 1A - Recapitulation of all Premiums
Underwriting and Investment Exhibit - Part 1B - Premiums Written
Underwriting and Investment Exhibit - Part 2 - Losses Paid and Incurred
Underwriting and Investment Exhibit - Part 2A - Unpaid Losses and Loss Adjustment Expenses
Underwriting and Investment Exhibit - Part 3 - Expenses
Exhibit of Net Investment Income
Exhibit of Capital Gains (Losses)
Exhibit 1 - Analysis of Non-Admitted Assets and Related Items
Notes to Financial Statements
General Interrogatories - Part 1 - General
General Interrogatories - Part 1 - Board of Directors
General Interrogatories - Part 1 - Financial
General Interrogatories - Part 1 - Investment
General Interrogatories - Part 1 - Other
General Interrogatories - Part 2
Five-Year Historical Data
Exhibit of Premiums and Losses
Schedule F - Part 1
Schedule F - Part 2
Schedule F - Part 3
Schedule F - Part 4
Schedule F - Part 5
Schedule F - Part 5 - Bank Footnote

Schedule F - Part 6 - Section 1 - Provision for Reinsurance Ceded to Certified Reinsurers
Schedule F - Part 6 - Section 1 - Bank Footnote
Schedule F - Part 6 - Section 2 - Provision for Overdue Reinsurance Ceded to Certified Reinsurers
Schedule F - Part 7 - Provision for Overdue Authorized Reinsurance
Schedule F - Part 8 - Provision for Overdue Reinsurance
Schedule F - Part 9 - Restatement of Balance Sheet to Identify Net Credit for Reinsurance
Schedule H - Part 1
Schedule H - Part 2 - Reserves and Liabilities
Schedule H - Part 3 - Prior Year's Claim Reserves and Liabilities
Schedule H - Part 4 - Reinsurance
Schedule H - Part 5 - Health Claims
Schedule P - Part 1 - Summary
Schedule P - Part 2 - Summary
Schedule P - Part 3 - Summary
Schedule P - Part 4 - Summary
Schedule P - Part 1A - Homeowners/Farmowners
Schedule P - Part 1B - Private Passenger Auto Liability/Medical
Schedule P - Part 1C - Commercial Auto/Truck Liability/Medical
Schedule P - Part 1D - Workers' Compensation (Excluding Excess Workers' Compensation)
Schedule P - Part 1E - Commercial Multiple Peril
Schedule P - Part 1F - Section 1 - Medical Professional Liability - Occurrence
Schedule P - Part 1F - Section 2 - Medical Professional Liability - Claims-Made
Schedule P - Part 1G - Special Liability (Ocean Marine, Aircraft (all perils), Boiler and Machinery)
Schedule P - Part 1H - Section 1 - Other Liability - Occurrence
Schedule P - Part 1H - Section 2 - Other Liability - Claims-Made
Schedule P - Part 1I - Special Property (Fire, Allied Lines...)
Schedule P - Part 1J - Auto Physical Damage
Schedule P - Part 1K - Fidelity/Surety
Schedule P - Part 1L - Other (Including Credit, Accident and Health)
Schedule P - Part 1M - International
Schedule P - Part 1N - Reinsurance - Nonproportional Assumed Property
Schedule P - Part 1O - Reinsurance - Nonproportional Assumed Liability
Schedule P - Part 1P - Reinsurance - Nonproportional Assumed Financial Lines
Schedule P - Part 1R - Section 1 - Products Liability - Occurrence
Schedule P - Part 1R - Section 2 - Products Liability - Claims-Made
Schedule P - Part 1S - Financial Guaranty/Mortgage Guaranty
Schedule P - Part 1T - Warranty
Schedule P - Part 2A - Homeowners/Farmowners
Schedule P - Part 2B - Private Passenger Auto Liability/Medical
Schedule P - Part 2C - Commercial Auto/Truck Liability/Medical
Schedule P - Part 2D - Workers' Compensation (Excluding Excess Workers' Compensation)
Schedule P - Part 2E - Commercial Multiple Peril
Schedule P - Part 2F - Section 1 - Medical Professional Liability - Occurrence

Schedule P - Part 2F - Section 2 - Medical Professional Liability - Claims-Made
Schedule P - Part 2G - Special Liability (Ocean Marine, Aircraft (all perils), Boiler and Machinery)
Schedule P - Part 2H - Section 1 - Other Liability - Occurrence
Schedule P - Part 2H - Section 2- Other Liability - Claims-Made
Schedule P - Part 2I - Special Property
Schedule P - Part 2J - Auto Physical Damage
Schedule P - Part 2K - Fidelity/Surety
Schedule P - Part 2L - Other (Including Credit, Accident and Health)
Schedule P - Part 2M - International
Schedule P - Part 2N - Reinsurance - Nonproportional Assumed Property
Schedule P - Part 2O - Reinsurance - Nonproportional Assumed Liability
Schedule P - Part 2P - Reinsurance - Nonproportional Assumed Financial Lines
Schedule P - Part 2R - Section 1 - Products Liability - Occurrence
Schedule P - Part 2R - Section 2 - Products Liability - Claims-Made
Schedule P - Part 2S - Financial Guaranty/Mortgage Guaranty
Schedule P - Part 2T - Warranty
Schedule P - Part 3A - Homeowners/Farmowners
Schedule P - Part 3B - Private Passenger Auto Liability/Medical
Schedule P - Part 3C - Commercial Auto/Truck Liability/Medical
Schedule P - Part 3D - Workers' Compensation (Excluding Excess Workers' Compensation)
Schedule P - Part 3E - Commercial Multiple Peril
Schedule P - Part 3F - Section 1 - Medical Professional Liability - Occurrence
Schedule P - Part 3F - Section 2 - Medical Professional Liability - Claims-Made
Schedule P - Part 3G - Special Liability
Schedule P - Part 3H - Section 1 - Other Liability - Occurrence
Schedule P - Part 3H - Section 2 - Other Liability - Claims-Made
Schedule P - Part 3I - Special Property
Schedule P - Part 3J - Auto Physical Damage
Schedule P - Part 3K - Fidelity/Surety
Schedule P - Part 3L - Other (Including Credit, Accident and Health)
Schedule P - Part 3M - International
Schedule P - Part 3N - Reinsurance - Nonproportional Assumed Property
Schedule P - Part 3O - Reinsurance - Nonproportional Assumed Liability
Schedule P - Part 3P - Reinsurance - Nonproportional Assumed Financial Lines
Schedule P - Part 3R - Section 1 - Product Liability - Occurrence
Schedule P - Part 3R - Section 2 - Product Liability - Claims-Made
Schedule P - Part 3S - Financial Guaranty/Mortgage Guaranty
Schedule P - Part 3T - Warranty
Schedule P - Part 4A - Homeowners/Farmowners
Schedule P - Part 4B - Private Passenger Auto Liability/Medical
Schedule P - Part 4C - Commercial Auto/Truck Liability/Medical
Schedule P - Part 4D - Workers' Compensation (Excluding Excess Workers' Compensation)
Schedule P - Part 4E - Commercial Multiple Peril

Schedule P - Part 4F - Section 1 - Medical Professional Liability - Occurrence
Schedule P - Part 4F - Section 2 - Medical Professional Liability - Claims-Made
Schedule P - Part 4G - Special Liability
Schedule P - Part 4H - Section 1 - Other Liability - Occurrence
Schedule P - Part 4H - Section 2 - Other Liability - Claims-Made
Schedule P - Part 4I - Special Property
Schedule P - Part 4J - Auto Physical Damage
Schedule P - Part 4K - Fidelity/Surety
Schedule P - Part 4L - Other (Including Credit, Accident and Health)
Schedule P - Part 4M - International
Schedule P - Part 4N - Reinsurance - Nonproportional Assumed Property
Schedule P - Part 4O - Reinsurance - Nonproportional Assumed Liability
Schedule P - Part 4P - Reinsurance - Nonproportional Assumed Financial Lines
Schedule P - Part 4R - Section 1 - Products Liability - Occurrence
Schedule P - Part 4R - Section 2 - Products Liability - Claims-Made
Schedule P - Part 4S - Financial Guaranty/Mortgage Guaranty
Schedule P - Part 4T - Warranty
Schedule P - Part 5A - Homeowners/Farmowners - Section 1
Schedule P - Part 5A - Homeowners/Farmowners - Section 2
Schedule P - Part 5A - Homeowners/Farmowners - Section 3
Schedule P - Part 5B - Private Passenger Auto Liability/Medical - Section 1
Schedule P - Part 5B - Private Passenger Auto Liability/Medical - Section 2
Schedule P - Part 5B - Private Passenger Auto Liability/Medical - Section 3
Schedule P - Part 5C - Commercial Auto/Truck Liability/Medical - Section 1
Schedule P - Part 5C - Commercial Auto/Truck Liability/Medical - Section 2
Schedule P - Part 5C - Commercial Auto/Truck Liability/Medical - Section 3
Schedule P-Part 5D-Workers' Compensation (Excluding Excess Workers' Compensation)-Section 1
Schedule P-Part 5D-Workers' Compensation (Excluding Excess Workers' Compensation)-Section 2
Schedule P-Part 5D-Workers' Compensation (Excluding Excess Workers' Compensation)-Section 3
Schedule P - Part 5E - Commercial Multiple Peril - Section 1
Schedule P - Part 5E - Commercial Multiple Peril - Section 2
Schedule P - Part 5E - Commercial Multiple Peril - Section 3
Schedule P - Part 5F - Medical Professional Liability - Occurrence - Section 1A
Schedule P - Part 5F - Medical Professional Liability - Occurrence - Section 2A
Schedule P - Part 5F - Medical Professional Liability - Occurrence - Section 3A
Schedule P - Part 5F - Medical Professional Liability - Claims-Made - Section 1B
Schedule P - Part 5F - Medical Professional Liability - Claims-Made - Section 2B
Schedule P - Part 5F - Medical Professional Liability - Claims-Made - Section 3B
Schedule P - Part 5H - Other Liability - Occurrence - Section 1A
Schedule P - Part 5H - Other Liability - Occurrence - Section 2A
Schedule P - Part 5H - Other Liability - Occurrence - Section 3A
Schedule P - Part 5H - Other Liability - Claims-Made - Section 1B
Schedule P - Part 5H - Other Liability - Claims-Made - Section 2B

Schedule P - Part 5H - Other Liability - Claims-Made - Section 3B
Schedule P - Part 5R - Products Liability - Occurrence - Section 1A
Schedule P - Part 5R - Products Liability - Occurrence - Section 2A
Schedule P - Part 5R - Products Liability - Occurrence - Section 3A
Schedule P - Part 5R - Products Liability - Claims-Made - Section 1B
Schedule P - Part 5R - Products Liability - Claims-Made - Section 2B
Schedule P - Part 5R - Products Liability - Claims-Made - Section 3B
Schedule P - Part 5T - Warranty - Section 1
Schedule P - Part 5T - Warranty - Section 2
Schedule P - Part 5T - Warranty - Section 3
Schedule P - Part 6C - Commercial Auto/Truck Liability/Medical - Section 1
Schedule P - Part 6C - Commercial Auto/Truck Liability/Medical - Section 2
Schedule P-Part 6D-Workers' Compensation (Excluding Excess Workers' Compensation)-Section 1
Schedule P-Part 6D-Workers' Compensation (Excluding Excess Workers' Compensation)-Section 2
Schedule P - Part 6E - Commercial Multiple Peril - Section 1
Schedule P - Part 6E - Commercial Multiple Peril - Section 2
Schedule P - Part 6H - Other Liability - Occurrence - Section 1A
Schedule P - Part 6H - Other Liability - Occurrence - Section 2A
Schedule P - Part 6H - Other Liability - Claims-Made - Section 1B
Schedule P - Part 6H - Other Liability - Claims-Made - Section 2B
Schedule P - Part 6M - International - Section 1
Schedule P - Part 6M - International - Section 2
Schedule P - Part 6N- Reinsurance A - Nonproportional Assumed Property - Section 1
Schedule P - Part 6N- Reinsurance A - Nonproportional Assumed Property - Section 2
Schedule P - Part 6O - Reinsurance B - Nonproportional Liability - Section 1
Schedule P - Part 6O - Reinsurance B - Nonproportional Assumed Liability - Section 2
Schedule P - Part 6R - Products Liability - Occurrence - Section 1A
Schedule P - Part 6R - Products Liability - Occurrence - Section 2A
Schedule P - Part 6R - Products Liability - Claims-Made - Section 1B
Schedule P - Part 6R - Products Liability - Claims-Made - Section 2B
Schedule P - Part 7A - Section 1 - Primary Loss Sensitive Contracts
Schedule P - Part 7A - Section 2 - Primary Loss Sensitive Contracts
Schedule P - Part 7A - Section 3 - Primary Loss Sensitive Contracts
Schedule P - Part 7A - Section 4 - Primary Loss Sensitive Contracts
Schedule P - Part 7A - Section 5 - Primary Loss Sensitive Contracts
Schedule P - Part 7B - Section 1 - Reinsurance Loss Sensitive Contracts
Schedule P - Part 7B - Section 2 - Reinsurance Loss Sensitive Contracts
Schedule P - Part 7B - Section 3 - Reinsurance Loss Sensitive Contracts
Schedule P - Part 7B - Section 4 - Reinsurance Loss Sensitive Contracts
Schedule P - Part 7B - Section 5 - Reinsurance Loss Sensitive Contracts
Schedule P - Part 7B - Section 6 - Reinsurance Loss Sensitive Contracts
Schedule P - Part 7B - Section 7 - Reinsurance Loss Sensitive Contracts
Schedule P - Interrogatories

Schedule T - Exhibit of Premiums Written
Schedule T - Part 2 - Interstate Compact
Schedule Y - Part 1
Schedule Y - Part 1A - Detail of Insurance Holding Company System
Schedule Y - Part 1A - Explanations
Schedule Y - Part 2
Supplemental Exhibits and Schedules Interrogatories
Overflow Page for Write-ins
Summary Investment Schedule
Schedule A - Verification - Real Estate
Schedule B - Verification - Mortgage Loans
Schedule BA - Verification - Other Long-Term Invested Assets
Schedule D - Verification - Bonds and Stock
Schedule D - Summary By Country
Schedule D - Part 1A - Section 1 - Quality and Maturity Distribution of All Bonds Owned by Major Type and NAIC Designation
Schedule D - Part 1A - Section 2 - Quality and Maturity Distribution of All Bonds Owned by Major Type and Subtype
Schedule DA - Verification - Short-Term Investments
Schedule DB - Part A - Verification - Options, Caps, Floors, Collars, Swaps and Forwards
Schedule DB - Part B - Verification - Futures Contracts
Schedule DB - Part C - Section 1 - Replication (Synthetic Asset) Transactions (RSATs) Open
Schedule DB-Part C-Section 2-Reconciliation of Replication (Synthetic Asset) Transactions Open
Schedule DB - Verification - Book/Adjusted Carrying Value, Fair Value and Potential Exposure of Derivatives
Schedule E - Verification - Cash Equivalents
Schedule A - Part 1 - Real Estate Owned
Schedule A - Part 2 - Real Estate Acquired and Additions Made
Schedule A - Part 3 - Real Estate Disposed
Schedule B - Part 1 - Mortgage Loans Owned
Schedule B - Part 2 - Mortgage Loans Acquired and Additions Made
Schedule B - Part 3 - Mortgage Loans Disposed, Transferred or Repaid
Schedule BA - Part 1 - Other Long-Term Invested Assets Owned
Schedule BA - Part 2 - Other Long-Term Invested Assets Acquired and Additions Made
Schedule BA - Part 3 - Other Long-Term Invested Assets Disposed, Transferred or Repaid
Schedule D - Part 1 - Long Term Bonds Owned
Schedule D - Part 2 - Section 1 - Preferred Stocks Owned
Schedule D - Part 2 - Section 2 - Common Stocks Owned
Schedule D - Part 3 - Long-Term Bonds and Stocks Acquired
Schedule D - Part 4 - Long-Term Bonds and Stocks Sold, Redeemed or Otherwise Disposed Of
Schedule D - Part 5 - Long Term Bonds and Stocks Acquired and Fully Disposed Of
Schedule D-Part 6-Section 1-Valuation of Shares of Subsidiary, Controlled or Affiliated Companies
Schedule D - Part 6 - Section 2

Schedule DA - Part 1 - Short-Term Investments Owned
Schedule DB - Part A - Section 1 - Options, Caps, Floors, Collars, Swaps and Forwards Open
Schedule DB - Part A - Section 2 - Options, Caps, Floors, Collars, Swaps and Forwards Terminated
Schedule DB - Part B - Section 1 - Futures Contracts Open
Schedule DB - Part B - Section 1B - Brokers with whom cash deposits have been made
Schedule DB - Part B - Section 2 - Futures Contracts Terminated
Schedule DB - Part D - Section 1 - Counterparty Exposure for Derivative Instruments Open
Schedule DB - Part D-Section 2 - Collateral for Derivative Instruments Open - Pledged By
Schedule DB - Part D-Section 2 - Collateral for Derivative Instruments Open - Pledged To
Schedule DL - Part 1 - Reinvested Collateral Assets Owned
Schedule DL - Part 2 - Reinvested Collateral Assets Owned
Schedule E - Part 1 - Month End Depository Balances
Schedule E - Part 2 - Cash Equivalents Owned
Schedule E - Part 3 - Special Deposits
Accident and Health Policy Experience Exhibit
Accident and Health Policy Experience Exhibit Summary Part 1 - Individual Policies
Accident and Health Policy Experience Exhibit Summary Part 2 - Group Policies
Accident and Health Policy Experience Exhibit Summary Part 3 - Credit Policies (Individual and Group)
Accident and Health Policy Experience Exhibit Summary Part 4 - All Individual, Group and Credit Policies
Supplemental Health Care Exhibit - Part 1
Supplemental Health Care Exhibit - Part 1 - Other Indicators
Supplemental Health Care Exhibit - Part 2
Supplemental Health Care Exhibit - Part 3
Supplemental Health Care Exhibit's Expense Allocation Report - Description of Allocation Methodology
Supplemental Health Care Exhibit's Expense Allocation Report - Desc of Quality Improvement Expenses
Audited Financial Information
Accountant's Letter of Qualifications
Communication of Internal Control Related Matters Noted in Audit
Management's Report of Internal Control Over Financial Reporting
Relief from the five-year rotation requirement for lead audit partner
Relief from the one-year cooling off period for independent CPA
Relief from the Requirements for Audit Committees
Credit Insurance Experience Exhibit Cover
Credit Insurance Experience Exhibit - Part 1A
Credit Insurance Experience Exhibit - Part 1B
Credit Insurance Experience Exhibit - Part 2A
Credit Insurance Experience Exhibit - Part 2B
Credit Insurance Experience Exhibit - Part 2C
Credit Insurance Experience Exhibit - Part 2D
Credit Insurance Experience Exhibit - Part 3A

Credit Insurance Experience Exhibit - Part 3B
Credit Insurance Experience Exhibit - Part 4
Credit Insurance Experience Exhibit - Part 5
Credit Insurance Experience Exhibit - Part 6
Financial Guaranty Insurance Exhibit
Financial Guaranty Insurance Exhibit - Part 1
Financial Guaranty Insurance Exhibit - Part 2
Financial Guaranty Insurance Exhibit Part 3A
Financial Guaranty Insurance Exhibit Part 3B
Financial Guaranty Insurance Exhibit Part 3C
Financial Guaranty Insurance Exhibit Part 3D
Financial Guaranty Insurance Exhibit Part 3E
Financial Guaranty Insurance Exhibit Part 3F
Financial Guaranty Insurance Exhibit Part 4A
Financial Guaranty Insurance Exhibit Part 4B
Financial Guaranty Insurance Exhibit Part 4C
Financial Guaranty Insurance Exhibit Part 4D
Financial Guaranty Insurance Exhibit Part 4E
Financial Guaranty Insurance Exhibit Part 4F
Financial Guaranty Insurance Exhibit Part 4G
Financial Guaranty Insurance Exhibit Part 4H
Financial Guaranty Insurance Exhibit Part 4I
Financial Guaranty Insurance Exhibit - Part 5A
Financial Guaranty Insurance Exhibit - Part 5B
Financial Guaranty Insurance Exhibit - Part 5C
Financial Guaranty Insurance Exhibit - Part 6A
Financial Guaranty Insurance Exhibit - Part 6B
Financial Guaranty Insurance Exhibit - Part 6C
Financial Guaranty Insurance Exhibit - Part 7 (000) omitted
Insurance Expense Exhibit - Cover
Insurance Expense Exhibit - Interrogatories
Insurance Expense Exhibit - Part I - Allocation to Expense Groups
Insurance Expense Exhibit - Part II
Insurance Expense Exhibit - Part III
Insurance Expense Exhibit - Overflow Page for Write-Ins
Supplemental Investment Risks Interrogatories
Long-Term Care Experience Reporting Form 1
Long-Term Care Experience Reporting Form 2A - Individual
Long-Term Care Experience Reporting Form 2B - Group
Long-Term Care Experience Reporting Form 2C - Summary
Long-Term Care Experience Reporting Form 3 - Individual - Part 1
Long-Term Care Experience Reporting Form 3 - Individual - Part 2
Long-Term Care Experience Reporting Form 3 - Individual - Part 3

Long-Term Care Experience Reporting Form 3 - Individual - Part 4
Long-Term Care Experience Reporting Form 3 - Group - Part 1
Long-Term Care Experience Reporting Form 3 - Group - Part 2
Long-Term Care Experience Reporting Form 3 - Group - Part 3
Long-Term Care Experience Reporting Form 3 - Group - Part 4
Long-Term Care Experience Reporting Form 3 - Summary - Part 1
Long-Term Care Experience Reporting Form 3 - Summary - Part 2
Long-Term Care Experience Reporting Form 3 - Summary - Part 3
Long-Term Care Experience Reporting Form 3 - Summary - Part 4
Long-Term Care Experience Reporting Form 4
Long-Term Care Experience Reporting Form 5
Management's Discussion and Analysis
Medicare Supplement - State/Policy Form Information
Medicare Part D Coverage Supplement
Premiums Attributed to Protected Cells
Reinsurance Attestation Supplement
Exceptions to the Reinsurance Attestation Supplement
Reinsurance Summary Supplemental Filing
Schedule SIS
Schedule SIS II
Schedule SIS III
Schedule SIS IV
Statement of Actuarial Opinion
Statement of Actuarial Opinion - Exhibit A - Scope
Statement of Actuarial Opinion - Exhibit B - Disclosures
Supplement A to Schedule T
Supplemental Compensation Exhibit
Trusteed Surplus - Cover
Trusteed Surplus Statement - Assets
Trusteed Surplus Statement - Liabilities and Trusteed Surplus
Trusteed Surplus Overflow Page
Bail Bonds Supplement
Director and Officer Insurance Coverage Supplement